722067

$6.13

int

# Box Broken Open

## The Architecture of Ted Pappas

Tim Gilmore

with Mark Pappas

Box Broken Open
The Architecture of Ted Pappas

Copyright © 2022 by Tim Gilmore

ISBN: 978-1-949810-13-4

The Florida Historical Society Press
435 Brevard Avenue
Cocoa, FL 32922
http://myfloridahistory.org/fhspress

Cover design by Jon White based on a rendering of the Mary L. Singleton Senior Center by Ted Pappas.

PRESS

This book is dedicated, according to the wishes

of Ted Pappas, to Mary Lee Pappas

# Table of Contents

# Chronology of Pappas Projects and Designs
## Mentioned in this Text

1981    Banjo's Restaurant

1981    Youth Development Center for Boys

1977, 1981    Seminole Club Restoration

1970-1982    St. Photios Greek Orthodox National Shrine, accepted design

1983    Bolles School, Whitehurst Lower School Campus

1983    Bolles School, Football Stadium

1983    Bedell Building/Jacksonville Free Public Library Restoration

1983    First National Bank Building Renovation

1983    Beaches Branch Library

1984    Bolles School, San Jose Hotel/Bolles Hall Restoration

1985    Bolles School, Cindy and Jay Stein Fine Arts Building

1986    Epping Forest Renovation and Conversion to Yacht Club

1987    Edward Waters College, B.F. Lee Seminary Building Restoration

1987    Wilk Residence

1989    Bolles School, Olympic Swimming Pool

1989    Southeast Tape Company Building

1990    Bolles School, Lynch Theater

1991    Edward Waters College, Centennial Hall Restoration

1998    Friday Musical Reconstruction

1998    Old St. Andrews Church Restoration

1999-2002    Brentwood Public Housing Redevelopment

2004    Edward Waters College, Adams-Jenkins Sports and Music Complex

2006    Metro Jax Community Development Corporation HabiJax Prototype

2007    Bolles Bartram Campus Gymnasium

2014    North Point Town Center

2020    Edward Waters College, Community Field and Athletic Stadium

# Acknowledgments

## by Ted Pappas

It is both challenging and humbling to reflect back on all of those who have impacted my career as an architect. And the list is so much longer than I trust my memory to draw upon—the teachers I had, fellow students who offered inspiration and competition, and my fellow architects discussed throughout the book. There are the engineers, contractors—too many to name for fear of leaving someone out. Of course, without clients, the architect has no path to make his ideas physical realities. It is the greatest joy to work with someone to provide a solution to their needs, and to bring that solution to life. A number of projects are referenced herein, but so many more are not. And to those many clients I offer my sincere gratitude. I consider myself and my practice to be first and foremost a service firm. Yes, I love design and always welcome those commissions that allow my creativity to flourish. But of equal importance are those projects that needed complex space planning, that required thoughtful planning to expand a house or building no matter how small. To all my clients, thank you. You all have inspired, challenged, and provided opportunity for me to do what I love.

It takes a team to design, and I have been honored and blessed to have worked with some of the best associates and staff anyone could hope for. First and foremost, Jerry Brim has been a friend since our days as classmates in high school. We took different but similar paths into education and then the service, only to find ourselves back in Jacksonville, studying for the license exam together and eventually partnering when we were ready to break out on our own. Jerry was the detail man balancing out my big picture focus. He's as good a draftsman as you will ever find—I'd put him up against any computer program. It was having Jerry Brim as my partner that enabled me to devote my time to the AIA and give back to the profession I so love. Through heated conversations, late nights, lean times, and fighting not to drown when our cup was overflowing, Jerry was the most talented and dependable partner I could ever have hoped for.

I would like personally to thank the following:

CLARENCE CAMPLEJOHN
BOB WISE
MIKE DENNISON
DAVID HAYNES
DAVE FERRO
CHUCK STRATMANN
DAN HUMANN
HUGH MORRIS
JOHN REEP
DEBBIE HANANIA
MASON ALDRIDGE
CHARLES KING
JASON FORRESTER
JOE DAVIS
ED CRENSHAW
BOB WHITE
MARK PAPPAS
DATA SONAVAKER
RAY HEEKIN
CHARLES ACREE
MARILYN BAIN
MARY KATHERINE PAPPAS ACREE
CHRISTY PAPPAS GILLAM
JENNIFER PAPPAS
SUSAN SHULTZ
CHASE ALEXANDER AND ALEXANDRIA ACREE
MARY CAROLINE, WILEY, AND GRADY GILLAM
DORINA BARI

MISSY GRISSINICK
PAI KARTSONIS
RAUL QUINTANA

The associates and staff I need to thank are many. My apologies to the many I will inevitably forget to mention. And a special thanks to my sister, Tee Pappas, who retired from a distinguished career with the IRS only to begin a second, even longer, career working for Pappas Associates, Architects and PBV Architecture, and who continues to work with me to this day.

# One

## The First House, the Mountain House, Mom's Folly

### 1. *Of the Hill*


A house should relate to its site. It should respect its position and location, take its cues from what the landscape offers. Never should a house dominate its site, dictate its site, conquer its site. Of all the things Ted Pappas learned from Frank Lloyd Wright, this principle would remain one of the most important.

That means "on" is the wrong preposition. The right preposition is "of." If you have a hill and you want a house, don't put the house "on top." Make the house "of the hill."

When Pappas was an architectural student at Clemson in the 1950s, he devoured Wright's texts, read everything the famous Prairie-style architect wrote. Having first wanted to be an industrial designer, Pappas learned from Wright that design could be organic. He loved the work of Raymond Loewy, the French-born American industrial designer responsible for the looks of Coca-Cola bottles and vending machines, the Greyhound Scenicruiser, railroad streamliners, and numerous corporate logos from Trans World Airlines to Studebaker.

But Wright's ideas made sense to Ted Pappas the way something obvious but never before considered makes sense. At Clemson, Pappas argued with colleagues, backed his Wright against their

Buckminster Fuller. While some of Pappas's future work, like that of just about any contemporary architect, would reflect Le Corbusier and Mies van der Rohe in certain details, he saw their work as egotistical, always announcing, "Here I am!" Ironically, the great egotist Frank Lloyd Wright designed structures respectful of their natural sites.

Pappas was learning to "destroy the box," to cut the ends open, to reject the box as design and the role of architect as decorator of its sides. He was learning that a structure should ask nature what it should be and to follow the horizon, developing strong horizontals, but also determining its shape and its flow "from the inside out."

"Wright noticed that in nature, structures often build from within," Pappas tells me. We're seated in the conference room at the offices for PBV Architecture on North Lee Street in LaVilla, Downtown Jacksonville. Since he began his own practice fifty-three years ago, he's always kept his headquarters in the urban core. Pappas still works on new designs and historic repurposing. He remains sharp, driven, inspired.

He notes the word for "Spring" in Greek is άνοιξη/*ánoixi*, which connotes the spring opening up from the middle, "like a bulb. It's the way nature opens." So you let the structure open from within in the nativity of its location and that's how you design a house.

One of the professors who influenced Pappas most at Clemson was a young rebel with a bent for dramatic expression named Fred Bainbridge. Exuding wealth, Bainbridge was known for his collection of classic cars. Any time you drew a rendering for Bainbridge, Pappas says, you had to include a Jaguar, a Lincoln Continental, or an MG TC. Bainbridge designed houses like land formations with rooflines sloping to lawns and windows perched like lookouts in the hills.

What he most liked about Bainbridge, however, was his skill at drawing. "Drawing is what got me into all this," Pappas says. It's something he says often. "Bainbridge could draw anything and do it naturally and easily." Once Bainbridge watched Pappas working on a rendering and said he didn't like it. He spit on the tips of his fingers and smudged out the drawing, put the tip of his pen between his lips for a second, then started drawing rapidly and breezily over the ruins of the original. Rather than feel insulted, Pappas was astonished.

Bainbridge was brilliant, but unruly. "He was always having problems with the administration," Pappas says, "because he was so wild. And he was always getting drunk."

At Clemson, a constant topic of discussion and praxis was the relation of form and function. The Chicago architect, Louis Sullivan, regarded as the inventor of the skyscraper, had famously decreed, "Form follows function." The maxim seems simple enough, but in the late nineteenth century, it had radical implications.

The World's Columbian Exposition, one of the early world's fairs, held in Chicago in 1893, had spawned the City Beautiful Movement, best illustrated by the "White City," a temporary "city" designed by architect, Daniel Burnham, to house the exposition. Burnham's ideals reflected *L'école des Beaux-Arts* in Paris, with emphasis on neoclassical and Baroque architectural principles. The elaborate ornamentation and grandiose designs, incorporating columns, pediments, balconies, and statuary, spatial hierarchies and symmetry, ran rampant through the American architecture that ensued.

Sullivan's maxim, which he articulated three years after the Columbian Exposition in his essay, "The Tall Office Building Artistically Considered,"[1] intended a corrective to *Beaux-Arts* ornamentation. Suddenly, forms with no function were heretical to a pure true distilled architectural understanding. Wright, who first studied under Sullivan, took things further, saying form and function were one.

"In this movement against classical stuff," Pappas says, "forms without function were seen as phony because they didn't express the truth. They conveyed an inherited image of what was important

*3*

in Ancient Greece and its reimagination in the sixteenth century Venetian architect, Andrea Palladio, the most imitated architect in the world. "So Wright sought to integrate form and function, not have them separate in any way." Raymond Loewy had done the same, designing steam turbine train engines as beautiful in their own way as a flower was in its.

Thus it was that Fred Bainbridge approached Pappas one day, noting the "flowery Florida shirt" he wore and its shoulder pads. When he asked Pappas why he was wearing the shirt, Pappas shrugged. Bainbridge reached inside the shirt and ripped out the shoulder pads. It was a strange and dramatic architectural lesson, arrogant and presumptuous, and it made an obvious point to a young Ted Pappas, one he agreed with and never forgot.

## 2. Beauty is the Experience

Ted Pappas's uncle, John Louros, came from Greece, served food on picnic tables by the river, made a little money doing so, and returned to Greece to marry Ted's Aunt Alexandra. He brought her back pregnant to Jacksonville, returned again to Greece, and picked up Ted's mother and cousin from their island home on Samos, where the philosopher and mathematician Pythagoras was born in 570 B.C.

Ted always looked up to his Uncle John. When Ted was eleven his father died, and his uncle increasingly looked out for him. He took him hunting north of Jacksonville, outside the small town of Callahan, gave him a bird dog, and introduced him to a group of Greek entrepreneurs who hunted together.

During World War II, when Ted was in elementary school, Uncle John ran a restaurant called the Stratford downtown on Forsyth Street across from the Floridan Hotel. Aunt Alexandra worked as cashier and young Ted stopped by all the time. The sailors in port spent all their free time Downtown and Ted grew fascinated with their insignia patches. When he found out they carried extras,

Ted Pappas, late 1940s, image courtesy Dialekti Pappas

he'd ask for them. They always seemed happy to give their spares to this enthusiastic little boy. He grew his collection fervently and memorized and mimicked the designs.

"We all thought he was going to be an industrial designer," says Dialekti "Tee" Pappas, Ted's older sister. "He used to always love to design and draw cars. And he was always drawing. Always had been. When he was a baby, our mama would visit with the other Greek families, and she'd give him paper and a pencil to keep him busy. He'd content himself with drawing for the longest time. And I mean he was a baby."[2]

Tee remembers Ted as always being "ambitious," but also very loving. "Anything he undertook, he put his whole heart and soul in," she says. "When he was delivering newspapers, he went out and solicited new subscribers. The delivery boy with the most subscribers won prizes. He was ten or eleven years old. He won this beautiful vegetable dish, this silver insulated bowl we still have, and a coffee pot and he gave them to our mother for Mother's Day."

Later, just as Ted was about to leave home for Clemson, a moment crystallized, with Ted and his uncle and other family members standing on the front porch of his childhood house on Ernest Street. Uncle John told Ted the one thing he wanted him always to remember, as Ted headed toward an as-yet-unknown career, was the ancient Greek phrase, Παν μέτρον άριστον/*Pan metron ariston*, "All things in moderation," a principle often so difficult for creative people.

College influences would come through strange amalgamations of Army Reserve life and philosophers like Dionysian proto-Existentialist Friedrich Nietzsche, and post-Romantic Naturalist George Santayana.

When Ted was a little boy, he'd wanted to be a school safety patrol at Central Riverside Grammar School but coming from an immigrant family who didn't yet fully trust the institutions, especially those quasi-militaristic, of their new country, his mother objected. He regretted it and made up for it in the Army Reserves in college. He liked the military discipline at Fort Benning on the Georgia-Alabama border, liked bivouacking in the woods, saw form following function in Army jeeps.

He went through Infantry and Airborne, but decided against Ranger School, having heard he'd have to survive by eating snakes in the North Georgia wilderness. He'd chosen to attend Clemson while in the Reserves partly because The Citadel, the Military College of South Carolina, didn't have an architecture school.

In the Army at Fort Dix, New Jersey, a lot of West Pointers were graduating, people he'd gotten to know well. The Korean War was finished, and these graduates were some of the first advisers headed to Vietnam. Most of those men, Ted says, would soon be killed.

Ted and nine other friends rented a tall oceanfront house together on the Jersey Shore. One Fourth of July, about fifty people stayed over and camped on the beach.

At Fort Dix, he took a class on Nietzsche from a corporal who'd studied philosophy at Rutgers. Pappas ingested *Beyond Good and Evil* and *Thus Spake Zarathustra*, understanding the German philosopher as "pro-Christ and anti-Christian."

"That got me in trouble back home," he says. "My family thought I'd left home, gone to college, and been infected with strange ideas." Because he'd questioned traditional Greek Orthodox thinking, they thought he'd "gone atheist." He hadn't. One of his earliest and still most significant designs would be for his hometown Greek Orthodox congregation.

In fact, he's never stopped reading about Christianity, ancient and new, and its uncountable variations and offshoots. As in architecture, he seeks to find the true constant, the deepest root, phenomenologically, from all variables. He was always seeking the authentic, the truth, the depth, the core. He was waxing Frank Lloyd Wright with religion and the study of truth and truthmaking and spirituality.

The professor at Clemson who introduced him to the works of George Santayana had studied with Santayana at Harvard and said Ted reminded him of the philosopher. So Ted devoured Santayana's 1896 *The Sense of Beauty: Being the Outline of Aesthetic Theory*. Though Santayana was a Spanish atheist, he predicated much of his thinking and form on the Dutch Portuguese Jewish mystical philosopher, Baruch Spinoza. In the section "Preference is Ultimately Irrational," Santayana asserts "no good apart" from preferring it to "its absence or its opposite," or, "as Spinoza clearly expresses it, we desire nothing because it is good, but it is good only because we desire it."[3]

Where Santayana most clearly influenced Pappas, however, was in his thinking about beauty, as embedded not in objects, but arising through experiences. Not only could you not have a preference for an ideal or model of beauty, without having a prejudice against its opposite, but beauty was "pleasure objectified," so that an experience of beauty cannot be wrong, since it's personally experienced. But the Kantian Thing-in-Itself can have no intrinsic beauty, which instead arises from past personal experience and definition meeting some quality definable in the object. What's beautiful is not the flower, nor its scent, but one individual's, as distinct from another's, experience of smelling and seeing that flower.

And that's what architecture should be. The Thing-in-Itself contains no definitive existence. Nor does one's own subjectivity. How, then, does an architect create a space that best personally reaches and enraptures the individual, but also creates the space the individual heals from, feels at home in, and both wants and needs it to be?

How does an architect create a structure that's less structure than experience?

### 3. House that Feels the Wilderness

In the late 1950s, Ted Pappas was, as he describes it in 2021, "on a high with Frank Lloyd Wright." His mind was primed for that introduction and germination of ideas that is college, in its best sense, and he had the luxury of brilliant and sometimes mad professors who saw his potentialities individually and pushed them.

He studied under Harold Cooledge, who had degrees in history, chemistry, and architecture. Cooledge once told Ted in class not to get offended, but that all the ancient Greeks had married or been killed off centuries ago. *Ted's* Greeks weren't *those* Greeks. When Ted and several other architectural students rented a house off campus, their professors would come around at times "like they were buddies." They talked about drawing, about why and whether the Piazza San Marco in Venice really was the best urban space in the world. Cooledge told them that the Soviet launch of Sputnik, the first artificial earth satellite, was "the best thing to happen to the United States." Ted says, "We were suffering with a great deal of hubris and he opened our inquiring minds."

Thus came his first real-world architectural opportunity and his first house design. In his final year, he studied with Professor Holland Brady. Brady had grown up in tiny Tryon, North Carolina, studying for one year at Clemson before serving as an Army medic, earning multiple medals, including a Purple Heart, in France, Germany, and Belgium. During Pappas's class with Brady, a wealthy family from Greenville, South Carolina, approached the professor and architect and asked him to build them a house.

The Robersons of Greenville had combined resources with two other families and bought themselves half a mountain. Having finished internships in Chicago and Asheville before moving back home to Tryon, Brady made a name for himself around his hometown and would, for more than sixty years, design hundreds of houses and churches throughout the Carolinas. He told the Robersons in the late '50s he couldn't take more work than he'd already accepted. He recommended, instead, a star pupil, Ted Pappas.

"I started going up to the mountains with Ms. Roberson," Ted says. "They had a daughter and two sons, twins. We got to know each other and connected really well. We'd go up there on weekends. They had a jeep, and we'd look at the site."

This family he'd just met was placing all their trust in him to build their family a home nestled in the mountains in a way they'd define themselves, and as they'd imagined themselves. Again and again, they drove Pacolet Road through the trees and mountains and curves and heights. The family called the site "Mom's Folly."

Jane Roberson was most engaged with the site, and she liked Frank Lloyd Wright. She and Ted met several times in the hills and drew designs and discussed ideas. Virgil Roberson wanted to use old windows from far-away textile mills the company he worked for owned, but Ted thought they didn't fit the house as the Robersons had thus far envisioned it.

The Robersons had gone in on buying their half of a mountain, but the more time Ted spent up there, the more he remembered Frank Lloyd Wright and sought to build a house "of," but not "on" the heights. The windows did not fit the house and the house didn't rightly top the hill. And the secret was the stream that determined ultimately the site and scope and function and experiential beauty of the house. For years the Pappases promised to tell their children "the secret of the stream," but more on that soon.

"We came down from the top," Ted says, "from imagining the house on top of a mountain," and asked the house to fit the curvatures and inclines of surrounding hills, forever falling, again and again, forever rising, so the goal became the capture "of the beauty of this creek that came down" to the Pacolet River. Ted noticed four trees that seemed to situate where and how the house should relate to the waterfall. Now he knew what he needed to do.

## 4. Secret of the Stream

Ted Pappas was happy with his first house design. So were the Robersons. "I felt at the time," he says, "that I'd captured the creek more than Wright did at Fallingwater."

He was beginning his career while still in architectural school and he'd taken all his cues from Wright. He'd destroyed the box by opening it up. In fact, the house proceeds in steps, just as does its mountain site.

You come down to the house from above. Both ends of the house, between four-to-five-foot overhangs, look out through two stories of glass. The bedrooms open onto the upper level with a balcony, and the balcony looks down two stories into the open dining room and kitchen. From that level, you come down to the deck and then the creek. The whole house forms an addendum to the mountain as it makes its way from the road above, then down to the side of the river.

Ted designed the house with a flat roof, which somebody told him he was crazy to do, but it functioned as an early "green roof" with moss, another instance of blending with its natural landscape. The first roof lasted fifty years.

The Robersons used Mom's Folly as a summer home. Ted didn't expect this first-built design to come back his way again, but it did. A decade went by. Just as Ted and Mary Lee had married and begun having children, buying their first home on Genoa Street in the Jacksonville neighborhood called Venetia, Jane Roberson called him and asked if he'd be interested in buying the house. Virgil had suffered heart attacks and the couple wanted to get their estate in order. Ted said he'd love to buy it, but he'd just opened a mortgage.

So Ted contacted some friends and proposed a four-way partnership. One of his friends had played football with Burt Reynolds at Florida State University, then played professionally in Canada. He flew Ted up to the mountains in his private plane, which he then spent circling in the clouds when he couldn't find the

Mom's Folly, interior, photo by Mark Pappas

grass landing strip at the airport in Hendersonville. That friend's mother lent him the money and the four friends incorporated their partnership as Mom's Folly, Inc.

As time passed, as the friends and their families scheduled their share of time at the house each year, partners began backing out. By the year 2020, the Pappases owned the house outright.

Ted and Mary Lee's children grew up visiting the house, always wondering what "the secret of the stream" was. It's Mark's favorite place anywhere. He frequently spent Spring Break, summers, and Thanksgiving there with his family. He'd miss it more frequently in the late 1980s when he was in college and Ted was president of the Florida chapter of the American Institute of Architects. He's probably spent five hundred days of his life there, he says, and wants it always to be the place he's spent the most of his life other than in Florida.

Anne Kenyon, a well-known portrait artist in Jacksonville, came to the house and painted it and the kids. The chess set on which Mark learned to play is still there. When Mark was a toddler, he disappeared once at the mountain house, and they found him just steps from the main road trying to find his sister Christy's lost doll.

Sometime in the late 1970s, when the Pappases visited the house with their family friend, Doug Milne, they hiked across the creek— *What was "the secret of the stream"?*—to an old logging trail, then wound around until they arrived at the old apple orchard. Mark had picked up as many apples as he could carry before it started to rain. As the group made its way back, the way seemed longer than it had before, and Mark became afraid they were lost. The rain came harder and heavier. And he was losing the apples. One by one, they'd begun to slip away from him. By the time they finally returned to the house, Doug had nicknamed Christy "Princess," and Mark "Hiker," the name he still calls him.

There were campfire tales of "Jake, the One-Armed Bandit," who supposedly roamed these hills and woods, and always either just below the surface, or around the next corner, was that question of "the secret of the stream." Did it have something to do with Jake? Or with buried treasure? With some strange thing that happened here long ago?

*13*

"For years they told us that," Mark says. "'One of these days we'll tell you the secret of the stream.'" So when they finally learned the secret, as kids, they felt disappointed. Now, however, the secret seems integral to this most special place.

It's how the stream works as a metaphor for life. When you're standing on the deck and looking up at the stream, you can't see its origins. The stream starts far beyond where you can see it and "comes down into view from the unknown." It "whooshes down and, from the womb into childhood, it slows in a place where it pools." It stays there a while, then slowly moves more quickly. "And then it really picks up. It gets busy, moves faster and faster," spending little time with its surroundings, rushes, trajectory-blind,

Ted Pappas and Doug Milne at Pappas's inauguration as president of the American Institute of Architects, 1987, image courtesy Mark Pappas

oblivious to all but its peculiar momentum, then moves once again out of sight, "where it drops off completely into the dark."

Tim Gilmore

Notes to Chapter One

1. Louis Sullivan, "The Tall Office Building Artistically Considered," *Lippincott's Magazine*, March 1896.

2. Dialekti Pappas (sister), in discussion with the author, May 2021.

3. George Santayana, *The Sense of Beauty: Being the Outline of Aesthetic Theory* (New York: Dover Publications, 1955), 13.

# Two

## The May Street School of Architecture

When Ted Pappas left the Army, he left his post as beautification officer at Fort Dix, New Jersey, where he'd been in charge of repairs and groundskeeping. He mustered out of the Army in March 1960, the same day Elvis Presley did, and drove south through a blizzard, with a boxer dog his sergeant mechanic had sold him.

Frank Lloyd Wright died in the spring of 1959, two years after Ted designed Mom's Folly, a year after Ted graduated from Clemson. Ted had read everything Wright ever wrote. Over the next eight years, Pappas worked for several architectural firms in what people unofficially called the May Street School of Architecture, a collection of firms and offices near Five Points in Jacksonville's historic Riverside Avondale. Pappas first worked for Robert Broward, a talented Mid-Century Modern architect who'd studied a year with Wright at Taliesin, the visionary architect's Wisconsin studio estate.

Broward, famously both quick-witted and mercurial, descended from a prosperous and pioneer Florida family that included the passionate and headstrong Governor Napoleon Bonaparte Broward. He developed a reputation as Frank Lloyd Wright's primary Southern disciple, since architect Henry John Klutho first brought Wright's Prairie Style to the Florida swamp in the early twentieth century. He'd even write, in two quite different editions, the definitive book about his Wrightean predecessor, *The Architecture of Henry John Klutho: The Prairie School in Jacksonville.*

Broward designed the Unitarian Universalist Church of Jacksonville, bringing shaded sunlight into worship space through skylights over barrel vaults of native wood, circling walkways and decking around ancient oaks. His residential designs also similarly resembled pagan temples.

Pappas smiles, cuts his eyes to the side when he remembers working with Broward, says, "Broward was kind of wild and when he left with his girlfriend for Alaska for a while, he farmed me out to Herbert Coons."

Coons assigned Ted to a team designing the Atlantic Bank Parking Garage downtown. Also brought in from other firms for the project were architects, Herschel Shepard, Mary Louise and David Boyer, Bob Wolverton, Bob Goodwin, and Peter Rumpel. That's when a young Florida State University student named Mary Lee Bone started working for the firm as a secretary. They married in 1962 and it would seem like they'd always been together, as indeed, if you're talking about Ted Pappas *qua* architect, they have.

Mary Lee remembers May Street fondly, the architectural offices and art galleries. "It was an amazing atmosphere," she says. "It was a new world for me. Ted and all those guys were the first architects I ever met. I saw right away how hard the job was and how hard they worked."[1]

She pauses for a minute and says, "Now I know Ted didn't tell you this . . ." Post-ellipsis, she begins, "Ted asked me to dinner. Asked me to dinner and asked me to marry him. He asked me to marry him on our first real date. I did not accept, but I knew I was going to."

At work, she'd ask Ted to lend her books about architecture. They'd sit on Hardwick's steps and look at Frank Lloyd Wright's designs. "He was so inspired," she recalls. "He was unlike anybody else I'd ever met."

Ted and Mary Lee had two wedding ceremonies, in fact, one in the old St. John the Divine Greek Orthodox Church downtown, the other in a Methodist church. Mary Lee says her parents were supportive; that the person who had the hardest time accepting their marriage was Ted's mother, Fifika.

"She was, at first, really not happy for him to marry outside of the faith and someone who wasn't Greek," Mary Lee says. "In the early days, I'd be the only blond head in the church. A lot of the older women in the church were leery, but I worked hard at it, and they did get over it. His mother didn't speak a lot of English and I think she was particularly frightened at the prospect of not being able to communicate with her daughter-in-law." She says she understood that fear, that the two women worked hard at their relationship and ended up close.

Ted remembers days when several architects, or sometimes just Ted, Peter Rumpel, and Mary Lee, would walk from the office on May Street down to the Derby House Restaurant in Five Points. Peter Rumpel, he recalls, was "always an eccentric character." Ted can still see him, "tall and lanky," walking across Five Points with his Roman sandals laced all the way up his calves. At the restaurant, Rumpel would just order chocolate cake for lunch.

There were three larger architectural firms in the city. There was KBJ Architects, whose principals were William Kemp, Franklin Bunch, and William Jackson; there was Reynolds, Smith and Hills; and there was Saxelbye and Powell, started by elder architects Harold Saxelbye, formerly of Marsh and Saxelbye, and Jefferson Davis Powell. Then there were other independents. William Morgan, known for his dune- and mound-based designs, kept his office in a historic livery building he repurposed downtown on East Forsyth Street.

Ted Pappas went from Robert Broward's offices to RS&H briefly, then worked for Taylor Hardwick, who also housed his offices at the May Street School of Architecture. Hardwick and [W. Mayberry] Lee was the penultimate firm for which Pappas worked in his eight years at May Street before opening his own offices.

Hardwick had converted second-floor bedrooms of an old house into drafting rooms and private offices in 1955, renting the ground floor to graphic designer and artist, John Ropp, for twenty-two years. Hardwick's second-floor conversion sufficed until 1959 when he bought the historic house next door. He connected the second floors via twin walkways, one containing a glassed-in conference room and the other a design room attached to his personal office. Hardwick made no radical changes to the houses themselves, just built fenestrated space in between and walled the compound in with perforated concrete panels. He started a small interior design and furniture store, Atrium, Inc., on the ground level of the second house.

In 1962 Hardwick designed an Oak Street expansion for Atrium, which contrasted wide glass display windows with white banks of wall a third the width. Here Hardwick sold lines of furnishings like Herman Miller, Richards Morgenthau, Dansk, Prober, and Lightolier. In its expanded location, Atrium, Inc., throve until 1977. When Hardwick left the May Street area, he converted the first-floor space of his well-known architectural offices to a Five Points-area art gallery.[2]

Thinking back on working for Taylor Hardwick, Ted says, "He was impressed very much with precast, and he also liked folded plate concrete." Ted worked with artist Anne Williams who designed the glazed brick mosaics on Hardwick's best-known building, the former Haydon Burns Library downtown, currently the Jessie Ball duPont Center. At Hardwick's home in old-money Ortega, Ted Pappas and Anne Williams assembled mosaics from miniature samples of colored brick. "She'd say, 'Ted, hand me a bright blue,' or 'Hand me a green,' and she actually laid out the entire mosaics, both exterior and interior, in full miniature models."

Ted also designed a service-entrance gate on the Forsyth Street side of the library. The gate, made of Hardwick's glazed bricks, cantilevered on an offset hinge. It lasted for a short while, then collapsed when a truck backed into it.

The May Street School of Architecture was destined to dismantle itself. Mark Pappas says it was inevitable that this cluster of "very independent-minded people" would break apart. Robert Broward, Herschel Shepard, George Fisher, and Herbert Coons started their own midsized firm between the big firms and the independents, headquartered in Arlington. Coons then went to Tallahassee to work with the Florida Board of Architecture. Broward moved to an office in an A-frame structure on St. Augustine Road. Fisher left to form Fisher and Marshall in a converted service station, since demolished, on Riverside Avenue.

The last stop in this *bildungsroman* of Ted Pappas's procession from May Street to his own firm is the fourteenth floor of the Old Prudential Building downtown, designed by Kemp, Bunch and Jackson in 1955. That's where Harry Burns kept his offices and where Ted learned much of the business side of the industry. It would be easy enough, in the bright light of "starchitects" like Broward and Hardwick, to miss Burns, but Burns was practical in ways some of the most visionary architects were not. Ted needed that.

"He had good business and political sense," Ted says. He focused on designing public housing in less populous counties, which led to getting commissions to restore and later design county courthouses. Burns sent Ted and Mary Lee to the national American Institute of Architects convention in Washington, D.C., an experience that would eventually bring Ted to leadership two decades later in the Florida AIA.

Burns's architecture also influenced Ted, who liked the "sand tone" of Burns's buildings and the way he played with "forms and voids." You can see that influence in Ted's first designs, the small Jacksonville Electric Authority Credit Union Building, now the Jax Metro Self-Help Credit Union, at 30 East 27th Street, and the Nick and Georgia Megas Residence at 5403 Sanders Road in the Jacksonville neighborhood of University Park, Arlington.

The Megas House clearly incorporates Wrightean principles in earthly symmetry. Thin bands of floor-to-ceiling front windows stand between four wide banks of sand-colored brick to either side of two widely protruded, yellow brick stanchions, a set of wide double doors in the center, all capped with wonderfully wide Prairie-style eaves. The house opens with walled glass to a back courtyard centered on an ancient oak, giving it a feeling of privacy and protection from the front, but openness to the outside and sky out back. Like a contemporary take on the Moroccan riad, that traditional North African house walled at the front, it centers on the garden and courtyard. With the Megas Residence, Ted Pappas was developing his own architectural style.

Meanwhile, Burns introduced Ted and Mary Lee to the practical necessities of running a firm. "I started to get the mechanics of the business and the confidence," Ted says. At the same time, his home church, St. John the Divine Greek Orthodox, decided it was time to leave its original home downtown at Union and Laura Streets. It was time for Ted Pappas to start out on his own.

Notes to Chapter Two

1.  Mary Lee Pappas (wife), in discussion with the author, May 2021.

2.  Taylor Hardwick and Jo Hardwick, *Taylor Hardwick: 60 Years of Design* (Jacksonville: Taylor Hardwick, 2014), 46-48.

# Three

## St. John the Divine Greek Orthodox Church

### 1. *New Directions for Ancient Traditions*

He was a young architect whose parents had immigrated from Greece, and he'd been chosen to design Jacksonville's new Greek Orthodox sanctuary. It was 1968. It was Ted Pappas's first solo commission.

St. John the Divine's former sanctuary, with its three crosses and two fish scale-patterned stamped-metal onion domes rising over Union and Laura Streets downtown, had been built in 1902 as Congregation Ahavath Chesed Synagogue. When St. John moved in 1968, the older structure stood exotic and byzantine another twelve years until First Baptist Church demolished it for a parking garage.

Pappas, then in his early thirties, wanted to blend two ancient traditions and make them contemporary. On a warm November morning, half a century later, we're standing before the soaring columns and barrel vaults of that design on Atlantic Boulevard.

"If you look at the immigrant Greeks who came to the United States," Pappas says, "they took as their pride not only the Byzantine heritage, which is early Christian, but also their Ancient Greek heritage. Here, I was trying to combine the two."

Influenced by Frank Lloyd Wright and having worked with legendary Mid-Century Modern architects Robert Broward and Taylor Hardwick, Pappas reinterpreted ancient ideas. With traffic roaring behind us, he indicates how the façade emphasizes the vertical, with its high steps and tall columns, a contemporary expression of a classical Greek temple. Meanwhile, the church, having given up two onion domes downtown, wanted a central dome on the new sanctuary, but couldn't afford it. So Pappas made Roman barrel vaults modern by using reinforced concrete and cantilevering them over the entrance.

The building committee wanted the structure close to the road for visibility. "But I said it needs to stand back if you want it to be seen," says Pappas. "So we pushed the building back and we decided to elevate it twelve feet above the crown of Atlantic Boulevard."

St. John the Divine Greek Orthodox Church, 1968, courtesy Ted Pappas

Orthodox churches are supposed to face east, just as mosques are aligned with the *qibla*, meaning toward the Kaaba in Mecca. As St. John of Damascus wrote in the ninth century, "Since God is spiritual light and Christ is called in the Scriptures 'Sun of Righteousness' and 'Dayspring,' the East is the direction that must be assigned to His worship." But the church had bought a north-south lot.

Most of the congregation embraced the new design, but a couple of Jacksonville's original Greek immigrants resisted the new direction. Pappas remembers one church elder, who'd donated the organ, always faced east when he stood during services. "He believed the church was going to collapse because it wasn't facing east."

## 2. *Colors of the Islands*

"Ted" can be a nickname for two traditional Greek names, Theodoros/Θεόδωρος—meaning "gift" (dóros) "of God"—and Eleftherios/ἐλεύθερος—meaning "free man."

Ted was born Eleftherios Pappas. His mother, Fifika, came from the Greek island Samos, birthplace of Pythagoras, and his father, Phillip, grew up on the island of Marmara, named for its famous marble quarries. After population exchanges between Greece and Turkey following World War I, Marmara's native Greeks dispersed to the Greek mainland, Thessaloniki, and the United States. Centuries before, the island had been almost entirely Greek Orthodox. Today, Marmara is Turkish, close to Istanbul, long-ago Constantinople, then the Rome of the Orthodox Church. In Jacksonville, Florida, a little more than a century ago, Phillip met Fifika.

Now I'm having black coffee and spanakopita at Athens Café on St. Augustine Road with Ted and Mark. Our waiter's name is Herakles. He says it's a big name to live up to, jokes that he doesn't have a gym membership. Classical Greek names like Helen, even Aphrodite, are still common, Ted says.

Ted grew up on Ernest Street in North Riverside. The original immigrant community in Jacksonville lived either in Springfield, just north of Downtown, or in lovely modest Riverside houses along Ernest, Gilmore, and Dellwood Streets between Stockton and Margaret. "That's where you came when you first arrived in the States," he says.

Greek was his first language, but as the youngest child, he grew up speaking Greek with his parents and English with siblings. He worked on the yearbook staff at Robert E. Lee High School and wore one of those old leather helmets that looked like aviator caps to play football. The old oaks and camphors on Ernest Street sheltered his childhood landscape.

As for the blue and white of St. John the Divine's interior, blue light coming through the tint of tall windows on blue flooring and the marble white icon screen, Ted says that while the newer church building just consecrated on Beach Boulevard uses red for the blood of Christ, for this design, this son of two Greek islanders chose the colors of a Greek island church.

## 3. *Heaven in a Bleak and Brutal World*

In an Orthodox church, the sanctuary is considered heaven on earth. It's a point Ted will remind me of when we visit other churches he designed. Inside, the icon for the Archangel Michael swings back on a door and Ted Pappas goes behind the icon screen. From behind he opens the central door, and the altar comes into view.

The icon screen, or *iconostasis*, the tall wall that separates the inner sanctum from the nave where worshipers stand, the most important interior architectural element of an Orthodox church, reflects the ancient as much as Ted's design reflects its own moment in time.

When the congregation moved from Downtown in 1968, the icon screen, built by woodworker and cabinetmaker George Doro, came with it. A half century ago, the Greek Orthodox church in Jacksonville was half a century old. The icon screen is as old as the congregation.

Top and center of the screen a single eye stares out over the congregation from beneath a small cross. That eye is George Doro's signature. Doro is best remembered now for the George Doro Fixture Company Building, built downtown in 1904, which the City and private interests decided, against community outrage, earlier this year to demolish. St. John the Divine's icon screen may be the most prominent example of Doro's artistry surviving.

Pappas points to the life-size icons of archangels and saints in the screen. "It doesn't matter where you are in the world," he says.

St. John the Divine Greek Orthodox Church, 1968, courtesy Ted Pappas

"Greece, Russia, Bulgaria, if you go into an Orthodox church, you will always have the Virgin Mary with the infant Christ on the left and Christ, fully grown, by himself, on the right." While Roman Catholic art sometimes depicts the Virgin Mary by herself, in Orthodox churches she always appears with the infant Christ. Martyrs stand depicted in the stained-glass windows along both sides of the nave.

The altar is visible between them through the open door. While services are now conducted in English, a Greek Bible remains on the altar. It's the language, of course, in which the New Testament was written.

Above the screen, the smooth concrete barrel vaults that cantilever over the entrance out front continue across the ceiling toward mirrors whose reflections make the vaults seem to tunnel high over the altar toward infinity.

Behind the screen, Mark stands by the incense holders, which altar boys sway back and forth on chains briefly during services. "When I was an altar boy, this was one of my worst challenges. If you put in too much incense," he says, laughing, "you'd smoke out the priest."

While not as devoutly religious as he was growing up, Mark loves the pageantry and mysticism of the Orthodox faith. He loves the atmospherics of incense and blue light, of the Good Friday processions around the church outside, of Resurrection services on Easter Sunday, when the lights swing and the chandelier above the *solea* shakes back and forth representing the earthquake sprung by the Crucifixion.

He points out that long before theatre and art were their own secular cultural realms, art and theatre were the province of religion.

"In the years of the early church and in medieval times," Mark says, "people lived a bleak life, no color, full of death. Then you went to church and there was stained glass and gold and this mesmerizing experience. It was a heavenly experience in a bleak and brutal world."

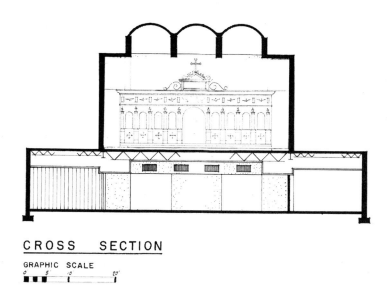

**CROSS SECTION**

GRAPHIC SCALE

St. John the Divine Greek Orthodox Church, original rendering, courtesy Ted Pappas

## 4. *Contemplative Architecture*

Mary Lee Pappas says her favorite of her husband's designs has to be St. John the Divine.[1] It's impossible for her to separate its design from her memories and personal attachments. It's the church in which the Pappases raised their family and the church where her children were baptized. Not only were she and Ted married in the original St. John the Divine downtown, but she points out that, since the previous church was originally a synagogue, the structure Ted designed is the first church St. John the Divine built for itself.

Other than St. John the Divine, Mary Lee considers the office Ted later designed at 100 Riverside Avenue, often now dubbed the Pappas or the Milne-Pappas Building, her favorite. She also loves St. Photios Greek Orthodox National Shrine in St. Augustine and Resurrection Catholic Church. She says St. Photios, on which Ted worked for more than a decade, "turned his hair white." The St. Augustine Preservation Board "seemed to want the Greeks to bring the attraction, but also not have any visibility."

Mary Lee remembers when Jacksonville philanthropist Delores Barr Weaver contacted Ted to restore Old St. Andrews Episcopal Church downtown. "Ted had always kept an eye on that church and apparently Delores had too. Then she contacted Ted out of the blue. She'd asked around to find out who did the best work on historic buildings."

Ted Pappas has always loved church architecture, both contemporary and historic. It's part of the reason his career has so often seemed to go in both those directions at once. Mark attributes this attraction to his father's love for the contemplative. Mary Lee suspects it also has to do with the way Ted's own church community looked after him when his father died, then "when he came back from college and they got ready to build their first church according to their own design, it was Ted they sought out."

In turn, through their father's design, Mary, Christy, and Mark experienced St. John the Divine as foundational in their own childhoods. They each list the church, along with the Milne-Pappas Building, as among their favorite of their dad's designs. Since the church was built the year Christy was born, the Pappases have always linked the two births on their mental calendars.

Speaking separately with both Mary Pappas Acree and Christy Pappas Gillam about St. John the Divine, both women depart at about the same place in our conversations to mention their father's drawing. It reminds me of Ted's sister Tee's saying he started drawing as a baby.

"He was always drawing," Christy says.[2] "If we were in a restaurant, if there was a paper menu or placemat, he was drawing on it." It's one of her earliest memories of understanding her father was some kind of artist.

"My dad was always drawing," Mary says.[3] "We'd go out to restaurants, and he'd draw on the napkins. For all our birthdays, for Valentine's Day, he'd make us cards and draw designs. Anywhere there was paper, he would draw. If we were in a nice restaurant and there were cloth napkins, it would drive him crazy that he couldn't draw on them."

Both daughters also discuss the fear they felt that this church, of all their father's designs, would be demolished when the congregation moved to a larger church toward the beach. "Losing that building would have been so painful," Christy says. "I just can't imagine what it would do to him, and at this point in his life and career."

## 5. *Saviors*

"If you had to ask me the best quality of this church, I would say it's the quality of intimacy," Ted Pappas says. I'm sitting in the balcony with architect and son in this otherwise empty sanctuary. "One of the same principles used in designing restaurants works here," he says. In restaurants, full tables in small spaces convey a different message and psychological setting than cavernous rooms sparsely populated at mostly empty tables. A church is a community, and Pappas's design reflects the historic closeness and fullness of the Greek community in Jacksonville.

So it was when the first Greek immigrants to Jacksonville held religious services in 1907 and when forty-nine Greek Americans of nine families and thirty-six single men attended Orthodox services at St. John's Episcopal Cathedral downtown in 1912. So it was when Father Michael Sarris prayed at funerals for victims of the 1918 influenza epidemic, and Father E. B. Papazisis performed weddings in 1956.

So it was when parishioner Tom Christon spent five years copying the Bible by hand in Greek in the 1930s, then donated the leather-bound volume to the church. So it was when Mary Roman compiled a three-hundred-page church history in 2016.

So it was when James Kalogerakos, having immigrated from his home village south of Sparta to New York in 1888, came to Jacksonville in 1901. So it was when he opened Riverside Fish and Oyster House at 510 Riverside Avenue in 1910 and brought his arranged bride, Angeliki, from Greece. So it was when, living above the fish market, they had five daughters and one son. So it was when by 1930 they'd migrated to West Sixth Street in Springfield and moved the fish market to Julia and State Streets downtown. So it was when James Kalogerakos, the oldest living parishioner, cut the ribbon at opening ceremonies for the new church in 1968. So it was when he died, one hundred years old, in 1973.[4]

St. John the Divine held its last services in the church Ted Pappas designed in early December 2020. Just before Christmas, the congregation met in its new megachurch campus on Beach Boulevard. Services now are in English. The new priest is Palestinian, though Ted Pappas says, "Father Nick Louh speaks Greek better than the Greeks." The church is diverse now—Russian, Ethiopian, Arabic. While mainline congregations shrink, St. John the Divine is growing.

While dedicated to moving to the larger space, church members worried about what might happen to the sanctuary Pappas designed, church home for half a century. Would the church stand empty? Would a developer demolish it to build anonymous and poorly constructed apartments? Would it meet the same fate as the church's last sanctuary?

Ahavath Chesed, the oldest Jewish congregation in Jacksonville, formed at Laura and Union Streets downtown in 1882. When the Great Fire of 1901 consumed the synagogue, architect J. H.

W. Hawkins's design rose on the same spot the next year. In 1908, however, the Jewish congregation moved, and the church became Christian Scientist.

When St. John the Divine, having first formed in private homes, purchased the building in 1919, Henry John Klutho, the city's most historically famous architect, converted it. When St. John the Divine left for Pappas's new design on Atlantic Boulevard in 1968, Metropolitan Community Church of Jacksonville, which the *Jacksonville Journal* called "a church for homosexuals ostracized by other congregations," moved in.[5] When First Baptist Church bought the newly declared historic landmark and demolished it for parking in 1980, architect Taylor Hardwick saved the onion domes. In a photo accompanying a February 11, 1980, *Journal* article, a dome sits on the ground and Hardwick stands beside it.[6] What happened to those domes afterwards is a mystery.

In the nick of time, at the end of 2020, unlikely saviors came forward to save Eleftherios Pappas's church. New worshipers will find it a holy space. This postmodern design, in which the son of immigrants made two ancient Greek traditions—the Byzantine basilica and the Ancient Greek temple—contemporary in North Florida, has been saved by a new congregation of Chinese Baptists. It's an appropriate next chapter in a trajectory that began with the city's first synagogue the century before last.

St. John the Divine Greek Orthodox Church, original structure, courtesy Jacksonville Historic Preservation Commission

First Easter services at the new location of St. John the Divine Greek Orthodox Church, 1968, courtesy Ted Pappas

Tim Gilmore

Notes to Chapter Three

1. Mary Lee Pappas (wife), in discussion with the author, May 2021.

2. Christy Pappas Gillam (daughter), in discussion with the author, May 2021.

3. Mary Pappas Acree (daughter), in discussion with the author, May 2021.

4. Mary Roman, "History of St. John the Divine Greek Orthodox Church," (private collection of St. John the Divine Greek Orthodox Church), 2016.

5. Patton, Charles, "Old Temple May Be Doomed," *Jacksonville Journal*, February 11, 1980.

6. Patton, "Old Temple," *Jacksonville Journal*, February 11, 1980.

# Four

## Starting Out, The Doty Building

Red Cannon operated other barbershops, but this one served as his political headquarters. Men of power stopped by for a trim and a shave and the scuttlebutt. Transactions happened, official and otherwise. Some folks needed a reservation. Others had a standing appointment. When Ted met Red, the architect was a young man, quickly discovering the efficacy of a well-placed introduction.

This three-story building was, after all, Ted's Uncle John's. It was crumbling. Then again, in 1968 everything in the center of the city was falling apart. If Jacksonville didn't implode in the next ten years, surely the earth would open up and suck the city down.

Clyde "Red" Cannon was twice City Council president, three terms chair of budget and finance. He cut hair and talked and listened and let things happen and made things happen. Certain things needed to happen for the city to go on functioning, but few folks needed to know the deals, the details, the details of the deals. It was Red Cannon who arranged to dredge Hogan's Creek, long a garbage dump for bottles and incinerator ash and factory offal and, once in a while, a body, so important municipal buildings, like the Duval County Armory, would not flood. It was quite a leverage. Red could lift a finger and let Mother Nature come back on the city.

In 1968 Ted Pappas was ready to strike out on his own. Having graduated from architectural school at Clemson and started out with the city's most prestigious and visionary architects, Ted found himself in a position with vision for his hometown. With its arabesque railings on balconies on the second and third floors, the Doty Apartment Building at Adams and Washington Streets had always reminded him of New Orleans.

In the building's present state of disrepair, you might stare up through the balcony struts and railings from underneath and think of Tennessee Williams's stage notes for *A Streetcar Named Desire*, how "the section is poor, but unlike corresponding sections in other American cities, it has a raffish charm," how the blue sky "invests the scene with a kind of lyricism and gracefully attenuates the atmosphere of decay."

John and Alexandra Louros, Ted's uncle and aunt, had owned the building since the mid-1940s. Ted was in grade school during World War II when his Uncle John operated the Stratford Restaurant downtown. Ted was eleven when his father died and, as much as he could, his Uncle John stepped into the void. When Ted started his own firm, he came to his Uncle John to open his first offices in this building.

By then, Red Cannon had resigned from City Council, having served, other than his time in the Navy in World War II, from 1939 to '66.[1] Cannon made a living and lots of relations cutting hair, and his nickname came from the color of his own. Lest anyone think it pertained to his political persuasion, he'd authored legislation in 1950 to make it illegal for a member of the Communist Party "to be at large in the City of Jacksonville." While the bill failed to say how authorities could prove membership, it specified that suspected Communists "at large" in the city, whatever that meant, could be jailed for up to 90 days.[2]

Red Cannon resigned when a grand jury probing city corruption recommended indicting him and seven other city officials for charging fake financial accounts, bribery, and fraud, including Cannon's acceptance of "unauthorized compensation." Meanwhile, cronies and colleagues came by for haircuts and a young architect shook hands with politicos and bigshots. In 1971 Cannon was acquitted, and a St. Petersburg judge with the improbable name of Victor O. Wehle (despite the jokes about "Judge Oh Well," the name has two syllables) said, "Becoming a little more familiar with the atmosphere of city politics in Jacksonville, I see nothing to be gained by putting them in jail."[3]

In its early years, this three-story masonry vernacular structure, first opened in 1911, housed Harris and Harris Grocers; Leonard Gill, Druggist; and Diedrich Rumph, Drugs and Sundries on the ground floor and two stories of apartments upstairs, where lived a tax collector (Edward Branch and his wife Nellie), a carpenter (William Abraham and his wife Clara), a cigar packer (Pedro Garcia and his wife Hazel) and a travel agent (Glenn Smith and his wife Lula); also various widows. The Doty blent into the neighborhood of two-story houses, apartment buildings, and independently owned businesses. In later years, it housed a Banner Food Store, DeLuxe Laundry and Dry Cleaners, and the offices of dozens of attorneys and physicians. The Doty was a community all by itself. In 2021, one-hundred-twenty-year-old houses still stand nearby on random streets, though the Doty stands alone in its immediate context, a reminder of the densely populated, ethnically diverse, and thriving neighborhood that once surrounded it.

By 1968 the city had condemned Uncle John's building. Says Ted Pappas: "So I told my uncle and my aunt, I said, 'look, I need to open an office and, if you'll let me, I'll run the building and collect the rents for you and have my office here, too.'" Because of that agreement, the building still stands half a century later.

*The Florida Times-Union* published stories about and photos of Ted Pappas "in his restored Washington Street office" in 1977. In those images, Ted plants a strong forearm on piles of architectural plans and renderings. He wears a short-sleeved, white button-down shirt and polka dot tie; looks up past heavy Greek eyebrows at someone out of frame. Houseplants hang in pots or grow up from floor pots before the brick wall and dark blinds in the window.[4]

Pappas at his office in the Doty Building, 1977, photo unattributed, courtesy *Florida Times-Union*

In 1978 Red Cannon died after a horse fell on top of him as he tried to mount it for a Civil War reenactment near the Olustee Battlefield, site of a rare late Confederate victory against United States forces advancing from Jacksonville near the end of the Civil War.[5]

Now, once again, the Doty Building deteriorates. The top two floors are painted brick red and the floorboards in the third-floor balcony have rotted away, leaving only the balcony struts. As is so often the case, it's painful for Ted to revisit buildings he's either designed or restored. Today, with the Duval County Jail and the Police Administration Building just a couple blocks away, the Doty and much of the surrounding district house bail bond companies and attorneys' offices.

Notes to Chapter Four

1.  "8th Jacksonville Official Indicted," *Tampa Bay Times* (St. Petersburg, FL), November 3, 1966.

2.  "Jax Commission May Forbid Reds Within the City," *Bradenton Herald* (Bradenton, FL), August 9, 1950.

3.  "Former Jax City Officials Sentences," *Orlando Evening Star* (Orlando, FL), August 24, 1971.

4.  Parks, Cynthia, "Arts Festival Architiect Designs 'Processional,'" *Florida Times Union*, April 20, 1977.

5.  "Riding Mishap Kills Politician in Jacksonville," *Tampa Tribune* (Tampa, FL), July 19, 1978.

# Five

## Resurrection Catholic Church

### 1. *Graceful Paradox*

When Ted Pappas first mentions Resurrection Catholic Church, he describes it as looking like a ship's prow. And it does. When Mark was little and his father was designing the church, Mark called it the spaceship. That works, too.

You'd think the church is concrete. Throughout the 1970s, culminating in his design for the Mary L. Singleton Senior Center, Ted experimented with Brutalist concepts. Yet what looks like concrete in his 1978 Resurrection Catholic Church is actually stucco. Plasterers gave the exterior a rough texture, not sand-finished, and the walls were left unpainted. From the rear entrance, the roofline starts low and tilts slightly upward, then as it approaches the altar and apse, the angles dart skyward, resulting in a corner centered on a series of tiered triangles pointing straight up into the cross on top. It's a graceful paradox: the church has the gravitas and the mass, no pun intended, of concrete, but it soars.

When the church was new, nearby church buildings, administrative and educational, hadn't been built yet, and the prow rose up through the pines. The site was tight. As you enter the church through the rear entrance, you walk beneath a low ceiling, "a space that is compressed," as Ted puts it. "If you want to feel the

Resurrection Catholic Church, 1978, courtesy Ted Pappas

space, you have to squeeze it, so we squeezed it down here and as you come into the church itself, it opens up."

Indeed, openness was a newly essential feature here. The Catholic Church wanted a different feel to its newer churches and it fit Ted's architectural philosophy. They wanted to open up worship spaces.

It reminds Ted of how Frank Lloyd Wright differentiated the role of the architect from that of other artists. "Frank Lloyd Wright said that an architect is a creative interpreter," he says. "Unlike a writer who writes or a painter who paints and the work comes out of their own soul, their work not subject to critique in the same way, the architect works for the party who's hiring him. That's an essential consideration." He concedes the irony that Wright treated his own designs like his personal canvases, growing irate when occupants altered furnishings.

Just as Ted always thinks of opening up the box, the Catholic Church was moving away from its previous strictly rectilinear designs. "There was a movement in a new direction here," he remembers. "The church wanted to get as many people as possible closer to the priest. The new kind of thinking was to get people close to the altar."

That meant that instead of the church extending in a long rectangular nave, it would fan out. Indeed, in an original hand-drawn rendering, the church resembles a paper fan. Ted looks back at that drawing and marvels at the work draftsperson Linda Mack did for the firm years ago. He notes that, in a rectilinear church, if it's big enough, you can sit way in the back and not even be able to see the priest.

The new goal of openness dictated the motion the ceiling and floor plan would take from the rear entrance to the altar. The slices of triangles that zig and zag gracefully in the ceiling are reminiscent of the theater's ceiling at the Singleton Center, but the movement of these angles is intentional. It leads you.

The amber clerestory windows above the congregation thrust forward at 60-degree angles. Likewise, the longer and thinner windows on either side of the chancel approaching the altar. Originally those windows, too, were amber but have since been replaced with stained glass. Just like the island-blue light in St. John the Divine Greek Orthodox Church, the amber of the windows here was important. There was precedent in Constantinople where Orthodox churches used amber-colored glass before they'd developed stained glass. Additionally, however, church icons nearly always have gold backgrounds. The amber has a radiance to it, but it's softer.

The entire movement of the design comes to its point behind the altar. Ted calls it "the crescendo, everything coming together, coming to the point up above." From an inverse perspective, that high-up crescendo is also the shedding of the light in radial lines down upon the altar.

Resurrection Catholic Church, 1978, courtesy Ted Pappas

Here, not only had Frank Lloyd Wright "destroyed the box," and not only had Pappas, but the church, decided to do the same. "When you have a rectangle," he says, "there's no particular focus. When you have a focal point, you have it at work both in the floor plan and in the ceiling and it all comes together at the altar. So the idea is that the focus increases and increases and the lighting brings you forward to the cross."

As is so often the case, especially with interiors, several aspects of Ted's original design have been changed. He's come to expect it; understands why it happens even if he doesn't agree with the changes themselves. Certainly, he never grows irate, like Wright did, but you can always tell that it stings.

The overall integration of the whole from each of its parts has been lost. He's particularly disappointed to see the altar he designed is gone. "The altar had a sculptural effect," he says, "with some of the

Contact sheet for Resurrection Catholic Church, 1978, courtesy Ted Pappas

same angles as the strong geometric form of the building itself. It had features that related to the overall plan." Original photographs show the altar cantilevering out on both sides from a central base, then angling up on both sides, the tall red tapestry rising straight up behind the tall cross.

*49*

## 2. *A Great Ship, Making its Way Among the Pines*

Ted used to laugh about how quickly the design of the building itself came together and how long it took to decide on the placement of the cross and the tapestry behind the altar. "That was the final focus and visual terminus," he says. "It's one thing to have form that follows function and another thing to deal with emotion in the focal point of the church. I recall they were talking about having the cross stand to one side, even though the symmetry of the overall design would demand it be in the center, and I agreed with where they put it." Now, however, the original cross is gone, replaced by a smaller one, along with the altar.

Sitting in a pew and pondering the changes to the design, Ted remembers the priest who was here at the time. After building committee meetings, Monsignor Eugene Kohls would invite Ted across church property to the tiny parsonage that served the church then. "He liked to smoke these Cuban cigars," Ted says. "So I'd come in and he'd light me a cigar. I'd start to smoke the cigar and then he'd pour a little bourbon. So then I'd have a little bourbon. When I got home at night, my wife would say, 'Who in the world have you been with?' and I'd say, 'The priest!'"

He notes the white sash that replaces the purple sash on the cross after Easter. I ask him about the differences in approach between this church and St. John the Divine Greek Orthodox Church a decade prior. Both designs unite ancient tradition with contemporary vision. The changes Resurrection has made since the design, adding statuary and changing the altar and cross, have headed back from the minimalism of the contemporary to the traditional.

Orthodox churches primarily use frescoes and icons, whereas Catholic churches use statuary, and in Orthodox churches, as Ted explained to me inside the Greek Orthodox church, the Virgin Mary is never depicted without the Christ Child. Ted mentions the distinctions between art forms and schools in the Middle Ages, how the Renaissance gave Rome and Florence artists like

Leonardo da Vinci and Michelangelo, creating religious imagery in unparalleled human form, while in Greece, the schools producing iconographers were centered in Crete.

"The idea in both churches," he says, "is that the sanctuary is heaven on earth." Still, unlike in St. John the Divine, Resurrection does offer views outside, but those views are to the congregation's back. While large windows let light into the rear of the church, the congregation faces away from the outside. The view outside is behind them. The clerestory windows above bring down the sunlight. "That was always considered important," Ted says. "You've left the world outside and you came into the peace of Christianity and Christ and wanted to be focused on him, on the liturgy and the mass and the communion."

Rather than a strong contrast between Resurrection Church and St. John the Divine, Ted contrasts both designs to Robert Broward's Unitarian Universalist Church of Jacksonville. "Broward, predominantly following Wright's philosophy, focused on nature," he says. "God was nature. Broward felt that. And that makes sense in a Unitarian Universalist context. In Broward's church, you feel nature all around you. And Wright said he believed in God if you spelled it nature."

Ted adds, "Here, you can bring the outside in from behind, but not in front. You didn't see it before you. Here nature is behind you. You leave nature behind."

Outside again, we've rejoined the world, but even here the ship's prow design of the church represents a distinction from the world. Not only does Jesus say in Matthew 4:19, "Follow me and I will make you fishers of men," not only is the Anchored Cross, or Cross of Hope, an ancient symbol related to Hebrews 6:19, which calls "hope" the "anchor of the soul," but the ship represents the church tossed about on the roiling depths of the ocean that is the world.

Ted didn't set out to design a church in the shape of a ship. The ship's prow manifested itself. He was "playing with form," as usual, working as requested toward a design to get as many people closer to the altar as possible, and the ship emerged as from a fog, a giant prow making its way among the pines.

Resurrection Catholic Church, 1978, courtesy Ted Pappas

# Six

## St. Photios Greek Orthodox National Shrine

### 1. *How the Shrine Envelops You*

The magic of St. Photios Greek Orthodox National Shrine in St. Augustine is the way it makes harmony of oppositions. It uses the box, breaks it open—as one of Ted's favorite sayings has it— then makes of it a frame for its interior arches. Specifically, that box is the reconstructed Avero House, one of a handful of houses true to their original form remaining in St. Augustine's historic district that predate 1821, when Florida first became a territory of the United States. Several dates for the Avero House get thrown around, ranging from 1702 to 1749, but the National Register of Historic Places goes with the latter. More pertinent to the placement of the shrine here in 1982, the Avero House was the place in St. Augustine where Greeks first worshipped.

The shrine uses several of Ted Pappas's favorite themes. Not only does he love the box broken open and the arch, but he's fascinated with intimate scale and loves to combine forward-thinking design with a deep appreciation of the past. His design for St. John the Divine Greek Orthodox Church demonstrates that most masterfully, but it's arguably St. Photios that captures that duality best.

Of all Pappas's designs, it's also one of the best examples of placemaking. Deep inside the shrine, standing in the chapel, it's hard to believe that St. George Street, with its hundreds of tourists buying postcards, sunglasses, and Panama hats, is right outside.

Tracking the way into the shrine illustrates the point. From St. George Street, you enter not immediately into the building, but through a door into the courtyard. In the garrison style of architecture represented by St. Augustine's colonial houses, you never enter a house directly from the street. The door, recessed in a wall of stucco, opens into a courtyard with high walls, which winds you around toward the entrance. Already, your way into the shrine has become anything but straightforward.

From the courtyard, you turn left toward the entrance of the shrine, then left again to enter the gift shop. Once inside, you'll turn right, then right again before you approach the chapel itself. What's the effect of all this winding? Instead of just walking in through a door that heads straight back to the chapel, you're wound

St. Photios Greek Orthodox National Shrine, St. Augustine, 1982

St. Photios Greek Orthodox National Shrine, St. Augustine, 1982

into the shrine, you're enveloped, you're implicated. Getting to the shrine is a process, slightly labyrinthine. You're involved.

Ted frequently notes that motion is a central element, a *material*, in good architecture. In the Mary L. Singleton Senior Center, he works on a grid with no right angles, so motion is material and the building's Brutalist concrete is not concretized, but pours, flows. In St. Photios, which at first glance could hardly be more different than the Singleton Senior Center, the motion incorporated makes entering the shrine an experience. Rather than a linear coming-to, you walk an arc, then switchback and walk an opposing arc, so that entering the shrine is a small pilgrimage.

Implication. Involvement. These words are not accidents. The way into the shrine *implicates* you, because the prefix *en-/in-/im-* means the preposition "in," and the root *plek* means "to plait" or "to fold." The design folds you into it. Coming into the shrine *involves* you, because the root word *wel* means "to turn," with, according to etymonline.com, "derivatives referred to curved, enclosing objects," leading to words like the Old English *weoloc* for "whelk, a spiral shelled mollusk," *vulva, revolve,* and *involve.*

When you finally come to the chapel, the relationship between words like *implication* and *involvement* makes a new kind of sense, because the chapel feels womblike. It feels safe here, sheltering, sacred. It's the rounded central space with the frame of sharp angles outside it. The chapel is arches within angles, curves within corners. You've come around to come to it and it feels like you've gone a considerable distance and dropped to a distinctly protective depth. How different the experience of this shrine would be if you walked straight into it from the street!

It's a sanctuary in that truest sense. It's both private and holy and it's a place of refuge. You can "claim sanctuary" here. Indeed, even the historical meaning of that word bears upon this experience. After the fall of the (Western) Roman Empire, European churches maintained the function of protecting the violator of *secular* law. The *sacred* was a separate realm from the *secular,* and *secular* rules would not necessarily apply to a *sacred* realm. Having been involved into this separate place, we each receive *refuge.* We are each both a pilgrim and a refugee.

There's another way St. Photios brings together what might otherwise seem opposite objectives in Pappas's architecture. So much of his work, as Mark Pappas often points out, focuses on spaces of contemplation like libraries and churches. Yet in listening to Ted discuss his *inspiration* (etymologically, not just the breathing in, but the receiving of the spirit of something: in-*spirit*-ation), you hear the *influence* (etymologically, the flow or motion inward) of the organic.

Ted designs a building to be *of* its site, not *on* it. He plays with arches, the Golden Rectangle, and spirals. The shape of a structure opens like the fiddlehead of a fern, it unfurls, it blossoms. The dualism in our thinking typically makes the spiritual and the physical oppose one another, but in much of Ted Pappas's work, the spiritual and the physical open into each other. St. Photios Greek Orthodox National Shrine may be the truest example.

## 2. *The First Greeks*

St. Photios Greek Orthodox National Shrine recognizes the arrival of the first Greeks in North America in 1768. On Saturday, February 27, 1982, Archbishop Iakovos, primate of the Greek Orthodox Church of North and South America, said, "This shrine is dedicated to those who came here 414 years ago."[1] It was at the Avero House, a decade after their arrival in North America, that the Greek colonists first worshipped. They'd rebelled against Andrew Turnbull's rule at New Smyrna, Florida, then marched nearly seventy miles up the King's Road to the Spanish city.

Turnbull, a Scottish physician and friend of British East Florida Governor James Grant, had brought thirteen hundred Menorcans ("Minorcans," in the spelling of the time) and Greeks to work for him at his plantation, which he named for Smyrna, today's Izmir in Turkey, an Ottoman city where he'd married the much younger daughter of a Greek merchant.

The colony lasted only a few years. Hundreds of colonists died from disease, and about six hundred of them decided they wanted no more of Turnbull's brutal reign. Their rebellion brought them up the British road, built largely along a connection of ancient Indian trails, to St. Augustine. Since there was no Greek Orthodox archdiocese in North America, the Greeks worshipped in St. Augustine with Spanish Catholics. It would be nearly a century before the first North American Greek Orthodox community would be founded in New Orleans, and the Greek Orthodox Archdiocese of North and South America wouldn't be established in New York until 1921.

For years, restaurateur James Kalivas led a small group of St. Augustine Greeks who made the case that the Greek Orthodox

Church should purchase and renovate or reconstruct the Avero House. The church bought it in 1965 and began the nearly twenty-year process of converting it into the first national shrine of the Greek Orthodox Church in the United States. A fuller historical understanding of the Greek experience in Florida, and here at this house, became available through the publication of Epaminondas Panagopoulos's *The New Smyrna Colony, An 18th Century Odyssey* in 1966.

Archbishop Iakovos appointed Ted Pappas architect of the shrine in 1970. He'd completed the design for the new St. John the Divine Greek Orthodox Church in Jacksonville just two years before. Though the Greeks from New Smyrna had worshipped with Spanish Catholics here in British East Florida two centuries before, those St. Augustinians who thought of their town's history as Spanish and Catholic resisted the idea of such a major Greek Orthodox footprint on central St. George Street.

## 3. *Showdown*

It almost didn't happen. Seven years before Archbishop Iakovos dedicated the shrine, a dramatic meeting at St. Augustine's Government House rang with phrases like "Calamity" and "No Compromise." By September 1975, it appeared the shrine would not be built.

Ted Pappas's initial design seemed "too modern," too contemporary and, in fact, too Greek, to members of the Historic St. Augustine Preservation Board. Even as Pappas drew up different designs, according to their initial suggestions, political alliances formed on either side of the possibility of a shrine.

Photographs of Pappas's scale model of the shrine show the chapel, based on the Tabernacle, with an eye-catching exterior situated at the rear of the Avero House's courtyard, instead of the entirely interior chapel as eventually built. Both the Catholic Church and the Orthodox refer to the Virgin Mary metaphorically as the Tabernacle (in both The Litany of the Blessed Virgin Mary and The Akathist Hymn/Ἀκάθιστος Ὕμνος), since the Tabernacle holds the Eucharist, the Body of Christ, and Mary carried the Body of Christ within her as Theotokos/Θεοτόκος, or "Bearer of God." The details of the original model's arches, domes, rose windows, and central cross on top are both intricate and exquisite.

Even now, half a century later, Ted still speaks of the rejection of the original design with surprise and pique. He mentions board member Robert Feagin, editor of the *Jacksonville Journal*, for whom Pappas had designed a house, as being "on our side." Feagin, however, abstained from voting to avoid any appearance of conflict of interest. The proprietors of a St. Augustine shoeshine business who knew everybody in town promoted the project, and Elizabeth Towers, mother of Jacksonville attorney Charlie Towers, came to support it. Ironically, some local Greek business leaders opposed the shrine for fear of losing St. Augustine business.

St. Photios Greek Orthodox National Shrine proposal model, 1975, courtesy Ted Pappas

The political drama reached its crescendo in 1975 when Reverend John Hondras, parish priest in Chicago for twenty years before coming to St. John the Divine in Jacksonville, attended a meeting with a message from Archbishop Iakovos.

The September 19, 1975, headline in the *St. Augustine Record* announced, "St. Photios Chapel Plan is Rejected." The article led with the fact that "St. Augustine may lose the proposed $400,000 St. Photios Shrine," its completion planned for the following year. "Hopes dimmed during a 'No Compromise' meeting at Government House between board members and spokesmen for Archbishop Iakovos of New York City."[2]

"I'll never forget it," Ted says. "Father Hondras attended but was quiet through the whole session until the end. When the leaders of the meeting asked attendees for comments, Hondras said, 'I'm here to give you a message from Archbishop Iakovos in New York.' And he said, 'If this project doesn't get approved, we're pulling the Orthodox Church out of St. Augustine.' And he didn't say much more. That was about it."

Some context for that ultimatum is important. The Greek Orthodox Church had never before dedicated a national shrine in the Americas. Greek Orthodox sanctuaries and communities in Jacksonville and Tarpon Springs also represented important centers for the church in Florida, but they couldn't match St. Augustine. Since nothing was left of the Turnbull plantation, the Avero House was the oldest existing locus of Greek worship in the Americas. The archdiocese figured the town that bills itself as the oldest in the United States couldn't refuse the recognition the shrine offered it when it came down to the wire.

"The board suggested that efforts be made to find a suitable site for the St. Photios Shrine outside the downtown area being preserved in the Spanish colonial theme," reported Paul Mitchell of the *St. Augustine Record*, but the message from the archdiocese was clear. "Although neither Pappas nor Father Hondras held out hope for further negotiations between the board and the archbishop," Chairman John Bailey and Robert Feagin urged open lines of communication. "Losing the shrine," Feagin said, "would be a calamity."

### 4. *Into the Blue Light*

On the Friday afternoon when Ted Pappas and I visit St. Photios, we meet Executive Director Polexeni Maouris Hillier, who goes by "Polly" and who's served in that capacity since the summer of 2005. In the exhibit hall between the gift shop and the chapel, Polly explains the grand display of clerical garments.

She says His Grace Dimitrios (Couchell), Bishop of Zanthos, had already donated his priest's vestments and just donated his bishop's. Couchell served as the shrine's original executive director. "His staff is not here yet," she says. "What we have now is an archemandrite's staff." She asks Ted if he'll take a look at the dry well in the sacristy.[3]

Ted is my guide all along the way, until Polly kindly joins in. He's pointed out the *reja*, the defensive grille, on the windows fronting St. George Street. It's Holy Week for the Orthodox Church and the shrine is filled with the liturgical chanting of the Akathist Hymn.

In the exhibit hall, large Art Deco block letters, lines alternating Greek and English, spell out the Lord's Prayer on one wall and the Nicene-Constantinopolitan Creed on another. Pappas also designed the Wall of Tribute across from the vestment display. He walks along it until he comes to his parents' names, Phillip and Fifika.

Here's the anteroom Ted calls "the zig zag room," explaining, "The shape turns this way on top of the old foundation." When Ted and historic preservation architect Herschel Shepard approached the project, only the foundations remained. In 1974 a team of archaeologists led by the University of Florida's Kathleen Deagan conducted an extensive dig here, excavating more than 32,000

St. Photios Greek Orthodox National Shrine, 1982, courtesy Ted Pappas

artifacts, including a cross from St. Augustine's colonial period made of some kind of animal bone.

The shrine's mission statement says, "Americans of Greek ancestry may come to be refreshed in the wisdom and warmth of their cultural heritage. The Shrine is also a public place where all may come to honor and remember their own immigrant ancestors."

Indeed, Ted soon finds himself deep in discussion with a Greek couple from Tarpon Springs, the Florida town with a higher percentage of Greek Americans than any other U.S. city. The three of them immediately begin speaking in Greek. They discuss family origins back home, inquire about mothers' maiden names, and what islands those names are associated with. The couple says they first came to the chapel when it opened in 1982. Today, they're heading back home from visiting grandchildren in North Carolina.

St. Photios Greek Orthodox National Shrine, 1982, courtesy Ted
Pappas

I enter the chapel with Polly and Ted, move past the ropes and
around the altar, and then to my surprise, a back wall opens, and
we enter the sacristy. Polly is kind enough to explain the dry well
to me, saying, "Any water that's used to clean the chalice has to be
put directly into the earth. It can't go into the sewer system." It's
been leaking. She asks Ted about fixing it.

On February 23, 1982, Walter Putnam wrote for the Associated
Press, "The black robed bishops from various dioceses followed
Iakovos into the shrine, named for a Greek Orthodox holy man
who lived in the ninth century, intoning Byzantine chants." 
That "holy man" was Photios the Great, ecumenical patriarch of

Constantinople. Putnam describes "arches and frescoes of sky blue, golds and beige" adorning the chapel within.

Indeed those "sky blue" frescos contribute to the strange and wondrous feeling of extradimensionality. There's some irony to Ted's having entirely interiorized the chapel after the rejection of his original design, which placed it with intricate exteriors in the rear of the courtyard. An early isometric drawing shows these curves within the corners as a world within a world. Ted's ultimate design achieves that effect more fully.

When you step across the threshold from the cream-colored walls of the modern exhibit hall and into the chapel itself, you feel you've arrived at a different depth. You move through tiers of arches to a central dome with its pendentives in the crossing of the transept. Above you are Jesus and the angels, and that blue that Ted used to such mystical effect in St. John the Divine Greek

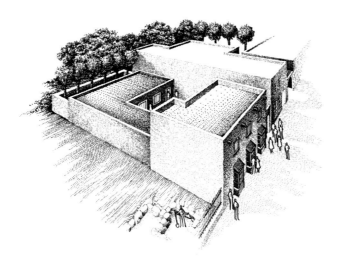

SAINT PHOTIOS SHRINE AND AVERO HOUSE RESTORATION   SAINT AUGUSTINE, FLORIDA
GREEK ORTHODOX ARCHDIOCESE OF NORTH AND SOUTH AMERICA

St. Photios Greek Orthodox National Shrine rendering, courtesy Ted Pappas

Orthodox Church. It's a sky blue, yes, but for Ted, it's always "island blue."

Often Ted oscillates between concepts like breaking boxes, playing with forms and voids, and imitating the shapes nature unfurls and the very pragmatic problems of lighting and air conditioning. He thinks "big picture," but he's interested in every challenge a project presents.

"So we had the problem of getting lighting behind the frescoes," he says, "and I decided we needed to use neon. You wouldn't suspect this is neon light, but it is. The iconographers don't like it because they say it's too blue." But Ted Pappas loves blue light. The blue light backing the icons of saints, of St. Photios and Christ Pantocrator, is the same blue light as in St. John the Divine. I find

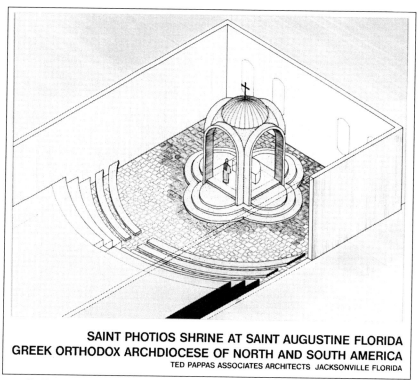

**SAINT PHOTIOS SHRINE AT SAINT AUGUSTINE FLORIDA**
**GREEK ORTHODOX ARCHDIOCESE OF NORTH AND SOUTH AMERICA**
TED PAPPAS ASSOCIATES ARCHITECTS JACKSONVILLE FLORIDA

St. Photios Greek Orthodox National Shrine rendering, courtesy Ted Pappas the signature of George Filippakis, famous iconographer and artist who's created frescoes up and down the whole hemisphere.

Meanwhile, air conditioning comes from corner vents hidden behind lower segments of pendentives coming down from the arch. You hardly notice the contemporary comfort in this seemingly ancient setting, but you'd surely notice the lack of it.

Under the central dome just above our heads, facing the altar, I ask Ted how he went about designing something simultaneously so monumental and intimate, so important both to worshippers and to clergy.

You always start with the space," he says, "and move into what needs to fill it. The space starts the whole thing. And, of course, you have to have the altar a certain size for the services to take place. So we had to cantilever it because the space is so tight. If you had legs at the corners, it would be awkward for the patriarch to maneuver around."

The apse feels just big enough to envelop the altar. And it's because of this tight space that even in this most traditional setting, one of Ted's favorite contemporary architectural features appears. The altar stands atop a capital atop the trunk of a central fluted column from which each side cantilevers.

When Archbishop Iakovos appointed him the architect for this project in 1970, Ted Pappas had just opened his own offices and kicked off his solo career by designing the new home for his hometown Orthodox congregation. When the archbishop dedicated the shrine twelve years later, Ted had recently designed one of Jacksonville's then most *avant-garde* Brutalist buildings, the Mary L. Singleton Senior Center, and a *Florida Times-Union* story referred to him as "one of the foremost architects of a new generation beginning to make their mark" on Northeast Florida.[4] Ted's wife, Mary Lee, says St. Photios turned his hair white. The twelve-year journey was Ted Pappas's own personal pilgrimage.

Notes to Chapter Six

1. Walter Putnam, "Greek Americans Honor Colonists," *Fort Myers News-Press* (Fort Myers, FL), February 28, 1982.

2. Paul Mitchell, "St. Photios Chapel Plan Is Rejected," *St. Augustine Record* (St. Augustine, FL), September 19, 1975.

3. Polexini Maouris Hillier (shrine director), in discussion with the author, April 2021.

4. "Ted Pappas: An 'Inside' Man," *Jacksonville Journal* (Jacksonville, FL), November 15, 1982.

# Seven

## Brutalism, Part One—Hogan's Creek Tower

The Jacksonville Housing Authority commissioned the fifteen-story, 209-unit tower in 1974. The Hogan's Creek Tower welcomed its first residents two years later. Built to house elderly residents with low income, the tower stands blocks south of where historically black and segregated Brewster Hospital and the historic wealthy black neighborhood of Sugar Hill once stood.

Pappas's Brutalist design echoes architecture like Le Corbusier's *Unité d'Habitation* built in 1952 in Marseille. Unlike Pappas's best-known Brutalist building, the Mary Singleton Senior Center, with its wall planks shaped on redwood forms with poured concrete, this tower rose from precast concrete sections.

You can read the rhythms of windows line by line, floor by floor, as if you're reading music. The apartments are modest but spacious, with views of the skyline that would dramatically raise the price of more commercial units, while out front stands a large red metal sculpture by Atlanta artist Carl Andree called *Jacksonville Trisect*.

A series of glossy photographs taken in 1976 shows several elderly black women at home in the tower, but there's no record of who they were. Who is she, wearing the crosshatched, cinched dress and horn-rimmed glasses, sitting behind her bed and beside her circular houseplant stand? Who calls her on that rotary dial phone beneath the bedside lamp? Does she call her grandsons?

In another image, she flips through a photo album, seated on that silk brocade flowered sofa, a framed graduation photo of a granddaughter or great-niece beside her. Ceramic dogs perch beneath the glass coffee table before her, atop which stand figurines of swans and chickens. In the view from her window, she owns the Jacksonville skyline.

HUD High Rise Apartment Tower
Jacksonville, Florida

Pappas Associates, Architects, Inc.
Jacksonville, Florida

Hogan's Creek Tower, 1976, courtesy Ted Pappas

The new residents of "the senior citizens' tower" praised their accommodations when newspaper reporters interviewed them. Many of them had lived without running water in their youth, siblings asleep side by side in flammable kitchens, wooden rooms built on wooden rooms in the deeper labyrinths of the inner city. Others had lived in boarding houses carved out of mansions. Now, in their old age, they'd come to this "poor man's penthouse," as some of them called it.

I can't help but wonder if this distinguished elderly woman might have been Frances Hines herself. Frances seized each chance to speak for her community. She needed to know each tenant to know how best to represent each need. She saw this vertical community as a neighborhood. The floors were the streets.

*Trisect* was the first public work of art commissioned in Jacksonville in fifty years. Most of Jacksonville panned it, but tower residents loved it, amiably debating whether it depicted an anteater, an elephant, or an ostrich sticking its head in the ground.

Newspapers said it wasn't "suited for the elderly people who had to live with it." That was the attitude of 1970s Jacksonville. The *Florida Times-Union* dubbed it "The Jacksonville Whatever." Carl Andree, then working on a three-ton metal sculpture for Atlanta's Central Park, said someone had suggested he come down to Jacksonville, put *Trisect* on a leash, and take it back home to Atlanta. He thought of his sculptures as "big toys, things that are fun to be around and to which you can react visually." If it stung him, as it must have, that critics, ever more vocal than supporters, seemed so rigidly unimaginative, vitriolically so, he did not say.

But the elderly residents of the Hogan's Creek Tower seemed far more open and gracious to *Trisect* than the typical Jacksonville critic. Frances Hines, seventy-one years old, ex-president of the Towers Tenant Association, loved her view of *Trisect* from her second-floor apartment. "I love the colors," she said. "You know, I'm old and I like red." She said she liked "the weathervane part around the eyes," which "tells us which way the wind's blowing.

That's alright. We get it." Tower resident Bill Harlow, said, "The vivid red is beautiful. I love it. It brings people together around here to see what the thing is."[1]

Notes to Chapter Seven

1. Leonard Ray Teel, "'Thing' for Elderly," *Atlanta Constitution* (Atlanta, GA), March 7, 1976.

# Eight

## Brutalism, Part Two—Mary L. Singleton Senior Center

It's an elegant paradox. Here, concrete feels natural as wood, lines flow like the trees in a forest, and the earth itself rises in tiers and terraces through foundations toward ceilings and skylights open to an overcast sky on a late February afternoon. For this is the house the earth built, and these are the forces, captured as material, like a photograph freezes light, that flow through the house the earth built.

The Mary L. Singleton Senior Center might be the only institutional building in Jacksonville built on a 30°-60°grid. Standing beneath hexagonal crisscrossings in the central hallway, Ted Pappas says, "A regular grid, of course, is 90 degrees and you can work with a 45-degree grid, but the reason for a 30-60 is that it flows. There are no square corners."

Near the end of the 1970s, three towers built to house the elderly rose utilitarian in the eastern downtown sky. Just next door to the Singleton Senior Center, Centennial Towers, designed by Herschel Shepard and George Fisher in 1974, brood dark over East First Street. Pappas had designed the Hogan's Creek Tower in 1976 and, in 1980, restored the abandoned Duval High School, built in 1907, repurposing it as Stevens Duval Apartments, independent living for senior citizens. The City of Jacksonville combined its goals of housing the vulnerable and aging and increasing the population of the urban core in the midst of decades of urban decay, suburban expansion, and "white flight."

That gothic exigency seethes in these designs. Yet all this new housing offered its occupants very little socially and recreationally, so the City called for a new recreational center to serve "senior housing" in the center of the city. Thus, Ted Pappas won the chance to design his most *avant-garde* and Brutalist building.

"We wanted to get the sense of a fortress on the outside," Pappas told the *Jacksonville Journal* just before Christmas 1980, "so it would create that sense of protection for the old people using it. Once inside, it unfolds and feels like a village. We didn't want walls separating people within. We wanted a sense of spontaneity."[1]

Outside, juxtapositions with nearby concrete buildings blare apparent. Immediately to the south, other side of Phelps Street, stands the Scottish Rite Masonic Temple, designed by Hyman Witcover and Roy Benjamin in 1924, and to the east across Market Street stands Shepard's and Fisher's Centennial Towers Building.

Unlike the senior center, which rises from and defers to its location, the Masonic Temple dominates its site. It's symmetrical and rigid, with a massive stone façade reached by steep monumental steps. With its Orientalist "Ancient Egyptian" motifs, the temple announces it's just that: a temple, a monolith. Ted Pappas loves the building's stark clean lines, though he makes the distinction, "This is stone that was laid as opposed to poured."

Here in the Singleton Center, motion is an architectural material. Concrete is organic in this Northeast Florida landscape of swamps and creeks. In this building, concrete doesn't weigh heavily. It flows. The emphasis is on its pouring. The two most-commonly used materials on earth are concrete and water. I never knew they were sisters.

And right angles occur rarely in nature. Natural growth curves and curls, spirals and unfurls. Designed on a grid with no right angles, this building incorporates motion as an element. Likewise, here sunlight becomes as much an architectural material as poured concrete. Concrete and sunlight both flow in rays. The light angles in from above, bouncing off 30° angles and 60° angles, and *angles*, as arrows of flow, become *angels*, since rooms contain no pigeonholes.

From high above, meanwhile, these geometries appear stellar, which makes the Singleton Center one of Ted's wife, Mary Lee's, favorite buildings, even though she says she might not choose Brutalism for her own architectural expression.[2] From an aerial view, the whole structure appears a series of hexagons, and their fragments like strange broken crystals zoomed in from outer space.

When an elderly man rubs loosely wrinkled fingers along the walls in these halls, he touches the shapes of ancient redwood trees, though he may or may not realize it. Their texture comes from redwood planks. Run your eyes after your hands across the flows of wood grain, the perfect imperfections of knots, the crevices and arcs. These walls are concrete poured onto redwood forms with gaps in between. After each pour, the ends are knocked off, the concrete redwood planks fitted together. Noticing the thousands

Mary L. Singleton Senior Center, 1980, courtesy Ted Pappas

of such details on these walls is like walking through a forest blind but touching all the variations in the textures of its trees.

The result is a Brutalism that grew like a forest. So often people criticize Brutalism as heavy and imposing, but each inch of these

Neighborhood Senior Citizens Center
Jacksonville, Florida

Pappas Associates, Architects, Inc.
Jacksonville, Florida

Mary L. Singleton Center, 1980, courtesy Tesd Pappas

forested concrete walls feels naturally dictated, designed. The eye touches the tree knots in concrete. The knots feel soft to the eye. Pappas's initial design hung trailing green plants along this central concrete spine, this hallway, and interconnected fountains in blue tile.

People hate Brutalism; people love it. Brutalism says, "I'll be here as far in the future as the structures of Ancient Rome are past," but poured concrete says, also, "I'm ephemeral. I appear inflexible and monolithic, but the aggregate I'm built of is process, just as the remains of the ancient past are both present and ghost."

The term "Brutalism" has nothing to do with being "brutal," so people who wish to "save" its legacy by renaming it "heroism" build their premise, like that of other "Lost Causes," on misunderstandings. The term dates to architectural critic Reyner Banham's 1955 essay, "The New Brutalism," and refers to *béton brut*, French for "raw concrete," and its use as material by Swiss-French architect Le Corbusier, archetypally in his *Unité d'Habitation*, built in 1952 in Marseille.

Assume that Brutalism dominates its surroundings and think of concrete as massive fixedness, and the number of ways the Singleton Center shows itself arboreal continues to surprise you. Not only does the original design accommodate standing trees, not only do the concrete forms show the natural formations of redwood, but the structure's geometry relates to the Kabbalistic Tree of Life, most often shown as a diagram built on hexagons, featuring ten *sefirot*, plural for *sefirah*, as channels through which travel the creativity and consciousness of an ultimately unknowable divine essence. The ten *sefirot* and twenty-two pathways of the Kabbalistic Tree of Life form one polyhexagonal figure.

And still, at the end of the central spine, the wide fireplace works as a visual terminus. You land your eyes at the very end of this central corridor and find this warm area inviting. Originally, the carpeting was the burnt orange of the late 1970s, the soft and cushiony seating similar to Eames chairs. With a quiet alcove off to one side, behind the fireplace, and a library on the other, the terminus, the end, the final homespace, is a large and accommodating community living room with a fireplace. It's the space that warms us at the end of life and welcomes us home. It's what's been there always and comforts us that it will be.

This is the view Jacksonville artist and activist Steve Williams describes when he says the Singleton Center is his favorite Pappas building. Though he sees the building's relationship to the earth, he says, "Something about it reminded me of a church, but also a spaceship. So many of his designs reminded me of some kind of outer space theme somehow."[3]

Similarly, Mary Lee Pappas says she loves the building because its walls feel like trees, while from above, "It looks like a star."

Look out over the terrace to the side. That old oak tree still stands. Two ancient oaks preceded this building on this site and Ted designed the outdoor decking around them. Even the foundations span over roots of the oak to accommodate the tree and respect its primacy.

Discussing the design for a December 22, 1980, *Jacksonville Journal* article, Ted described the shapes of openness. Like a Buddhist discussing form and void, he said, "There's a difference between openness in a field and containing space and giving it a form." He added, "The quality of a building is really the void itself. Not the positive, but—if I may make up a word—a 'formful' void. If you squeeze void, manipulate it, then it takes on its own shape."[4]

Pappas at the Singleton Senior Center, 1980, courtesy Ted
Pappas

Mary L. Singleton Center, 1980, courtesy Ted Pappas

Notes to Chapter Eight

1. Hugh White, "2 Pappas Buildings Win Design Awards," *Jacksonville Journal* (Jacksonville, FL), December 22, 1980.

2. Mary Lee Pappas (wife), in discussion with the author, May 2021.

3. Steve Williams (artist), in discussion with the author, May 2021.

4. Williams, May 2021.

# Nine

## Historic Preservation in the Urban Core

### 1. *In the Beginning*

It began in 1968 when Ted Pappas opened that first office in an old grocery, sundries, and apartment building owned by his uncle, John Louros, at Washington and Adams Streets downtown. Ted has kept offices in the building twice, from 1968 to 1982, at which point he opened new offices in the historic H.C. Hare Co. Building on Riverside Avenue, then again in the early 2000s, when the Florida Department of Transportation demolished the Hare Building, now remembered as the Pappas or Milne-Pappas Building.

Through the 1970s, Pappas expanded the firm's offices into the second floor of the Doty Building and renovated the interior. He replaced the original shotgun stairway with a curved stair with a landing. His redesign and repurposing served as a prototype for the graceful Riverside Avenue office redesign, one of his favorite projects.

The year before Pappas moved to Riverside Avenue, attorneys Hank Coxe and Jack Schemer moved their law offices to the first floor of the Doty Building. Coxe would remain in the building for three years, long enough to contract Pappas to restore the original Jacksonville Free Public Library for Coxe's firm, Bedell, Dittmar, DeVault, Pillans and Coxe, better known as the Bedell Firm.

Milne-Pappas Building, 1980, courtesy Ted Pappas

## 2. *Jacksonville Free Public Library/The Bedell Building*

Shakespeare's grim visage looks out over the doings of Downtown—the crimes and loves, the faith healings and betrayals, the intrigues of principalities, the farces fought between the rulers of the darkness of this world—as it has for more than a century. He's joined by Plato and Aristotle and Herodotus, the Father of History, peering through the stone acanthus leaves from the top of their two-story columns.

Charles Pillans III shakes my hand in the lobby, walks me to a conference room, and tells me what the library was like in the 1960s, before the Bedell Law Firm bought and restored it in the early 1980s. He's a short man, file folders tucked in his armpits, gracious and kind.

Jacksonville Free Public Library / Bedell Building, 1983, courtesy Ted Pappas

Pillans has been with the Bedell Law Firm for fifty years. He's been here a third of the time the firm's existed, and it's the oldest law firm in Florida. After the City moved the library from this original building diagonally across Adams and Ocean Streets to Taylor Hardwick's Haydon Burns building, the Bedell Firm hired Ted Pappas to restore its new home here.

One of Pappas's most significant actions in restoring the old library building was uncovering the tall, vaulted ceiling with the pinks and golden greens and blues of a Tiffany skylight in the copper roof. It had long been covered by a drop ceiling. Likewise, Ted uncovered the lightwell in the center of the second floor, which had been boarded over and stacked with books.

Charles's wife, Judy Pillans, was children's librarian here in the early 1960s. By that time, the library had become such a labyrinth of books that people could hide beneath and behind stacks of volumes without being found.

Charles says, "The place was so crowded, jammed up, chopped up, such a warren's nest that when it was cold in the winter, homeless people would hide in the stacks overnight."

The crime, Ted says, was the slow but steady application, decade by decade, of what he calls "maintenance mentality." Quick fixes pile up until, eventually, not only is the original problem lost, but so is the original vision.

Charles tells me how Bedell, Dittmar, DeVault, Pillans & Coxe, P.A., traces its roots to Union Army Colonel Horatio Bisbee in 1865. Bisbee soon partnered with George Bedell, and when George's son, Chester, joined in 1927, the firm became Bedell & Bedell.[1]

The firm retains the Bedell name, but no Bedell and, though it handles high-profile cases around Florida, it works only from this old library building in the center of Jacksonville. Four of its attorneys have been president of the Florida Bar Association.

One of the biggest challenges, Ted says, was digging down to the foundations to add space for junior attorneys. Meanwhile, everything that blocked the original Tiffany skylight, the existence of which surprised everyone, had to come down.

## 3. *The Seminole Club*

Ted Pappas was first hired for restorative work in the Seminole Club in 1977, and again in 1981. The challenge was to keep the club true to its feel as the oldest "gentlemen's club" building (before that phrase morphed in the popular lexicon to mean a strip club), but also to update an institution that in many ways, especially as it pertained to its traditions regarding race and gender, was already obsolete. Women wouldn't be admitted until 1988. The club closed a year later.

The Seminole Club began in 1887 as a prominent place for the city's biggest wigs, its top political and business leaders, to meet and dine and negotiate and drink and deal. The club building burned twice, first in 1891 and again a decade later in the Great Fire of 1901. Presidents and presidential candidates met here and just down diagonally in Hemming Park, now James Weldon Johnson Park. By the 1980s, it bore the now-dubious distinction of one of the oldest men's clubs in the country.

Seminole Club, year uncertain, courtesy Ted Pappas

Pappas opened up enclosed spaces within, restored the grand and complicated central staircase with its multiple landings and half turns, updated the bar and the garden room, a dining room with Windsor chairs, potted plants and floor-to-ceiling windows in wide bands, sunlight attenuated by tall, narrow, dark wooden louvers. Before the first restoration, the building had been painted dark brown, its eaves and exterior casings rotten, the upstairs porch enclosed with jalousie windows.

Peter Behringer meets me on the wide front veranda of the 1903 building that long housed the Seminole Club, originally designed by architect Rutledge Holmes. In 2014 he opened Sweet Pete's Candy Store in the massive downtown mansion. While it was still abandoned, he welcomed me into a grand foyer with Prairie Style leaded-glass lights pendant from a dark coffered ceiling. Coffered walls receded inward toward dark pilasters and a wide-arched fireplace.

Peter's is half the name of Peterbrooke Chocolatier, founded by his mother, Phyllis Lockwood, in 1983 and named for her children. It was Reality TV that enabled his business to move from a smaller location in Victorian Springfield to the Seminole Club building. Sweet Pete's appeared on an episode of the CNBC TV show *The Profit*, on which wealthy businessman Marcus Lemonis meets with entrepreneurs and helps turn small businesses around. Later Pete was the "quirky confectioner" with the "fun staff" on The CW's *Sweet Pete's: The Show*.[2]

## 4. *Duval High School/Stevens Duval Apartments*

One of Jacksonville's favorite historic buildings might not seem the recipient of much reverence. The Annie Lytle School, or Public School No. 4, sits behind Riverside Park, beneath an interstate flyover, at the boundary between Riverside and Brooklyn. Yet most teenagers in Jacksonville know the school for the urban legends that surround it and many young people have made what folklorists call "legend trips" in the middle of the night.

The school, built in 1917, was abandoned by the 1960s due, not to the cannibal janitors and murderous principals of urban legends, but to demographic shifts and looming racial desegregation battles. Plans to restore it have lifted hopes about its future repeatedly, only to fall through again and again.

Attorney Doug Milne, the Pappases' longtime family friend, formed a partnership in the 1980s to restore School No. 4, but it didn't pan out. Whenever skeptics call the school a lost cause, however, Milne's other partnership to save an historic educational structure, this one even older, begs to differ. In the 1970s Duval High School seemed headed for the same fate as thousands of other historically significant buildings in the urban core.

The Duval High School Building on North Ocean Street downtown is Public School No. 1. The original school burned in the Great Fire of 1901, but was founded in 1875, the oldest high school in Florida. After holding classes elsewhere, Duval High School inhabited a new red brick school building with limestone trim, designed by architect Wilbur Bacon Camp in 1908. In 1920 and '22, the school added wings with dentilled corbelling, balustrades, and arches designed by Mellen C. Greeley and Roy Benjamin, to either side.

Milne says he formed the group to buy the old building after the death of an unnamed client who'd attended school there. "You could take any other derelict building in town, no matter how bad a shape it was in," he says, "and this one was worse."[3]

In 1977, the *Jacksonville Journal* published a photo of Ted Pappas with trustees, Garnett Ashby and Dave Naughton, on the stage in the abandoned school building. When the building became Stevens Duval Apartments for the elderly in 1980, some of those high school students who'd graduated in 1927, the school's last operating year, fifty-three years before, became its residents. The school's last student, born a year before this building opened, died in 2011, one hundred two years old.

Pappas at Duval High School, 1980, photo by Rocco Morabito, courtesy *The Florida Times-Union*

Even the stand-alone annexes look as lovely as if they were their own individual buildings with their corbels, balusters, and arches. Ted points out the jagged cracks in the faces of the original structure. "Things settle over time," he says. He fingertips the caulking. Inside we meet an elderly woman dressed in all red, including her hat, seated on a motorized scooter, who insists on having her picture taken with him.

Duval High School graduate Bernice Walston died in 2006. She was ninety-seven years old. She was Bernice Richardson back in 1927. Her senior quote was "Blessed are they who have the gift of making friends." When she died, she'd earned a doctorate and lived in Athens, Greece, and the Canary Islands. In 1987 she

Duval High School, 1980, courtesy Ted Pappas

posed with her 1927 Duval High School yearbook on the school's original stairwell.

Duval High School graduate Martha Wells died in 2011. She was one hundred two years old. She was born the year the Duval High School building opened, she graduated the year Duval High School closed, and she died the very last student to have graduated from the oldest high school in the city.[4]

## 5. *First National Bank Building*

On our way from the Doty Apartment Building to Old St. Andrews Church, we pass the I.M. Sulzbacher Center for the Homeless, located at the old brick warehouse Pappas renovated in 1978 for Don Tredinick's Jax Liquors and General Trading Company.

First National Bank, 1983, courtesy Ted Pappas

Indeed, you could cross Downtown Jacksonville by throwing a baseball from one Pappas historical project to another. His historic preservation work, in or near the urban core, includes the oldest historically black college in Florida, the state's oldest musical organization, the city's oldest library, oldest private club building, oldest school building, and oldest church structure.

In 1983 Pappas restored the First National Bank Building, also called the Old Bisbee Building, at 57 West Bay Street, built in 1901 and '02 in the frenzy of downtown reconstruction that followed the Great Fire, and designed by Gottfried L. Norrman of Atlanta. Pre-restoration photos show a once-grand building topped by a balustrade with decorative urns and peculiar gables whose first floor had been plastered over, then boarded over. There's a "Durden for Sheriff" sign affixed to plywood in a window. In the section

First National Bank, 1983, courtesy Ted Pappas

east of the balustrade and underneath a gable stands the battered and grimy entrance to Valentino's Fine Jewelry.

Inside Pappas's First National Bank Building renovation, contemporary furniture against bared original brick walls and a sitting room off a landing, looking down to the first floor and out to the streets and the sunlight, echo themes and methods, the focus of the outside coming in through the inside working itself out, from many another Pappas project, whether new design or historic repurposing.

Another photo shows the rooftop balustrade against the glass of the Independent Life Building across the street, then the tallest building in the city, with an emphasis on floral ornamentation beneath dentilled cornice, including alternating repetitions of anthemion/ανθέμιον, the palmette motif with radiating petals so often found on the antefix in Ancient Greek and Roman architecture, which Ted made the symbol for his firm and used directly in his Beaches Library design of the same year.

## 6. *Friday Musicale*

The firebomb lobbed into the Friday Musicale burnt down the old building but couldn't end the music. This work wasn't a restoration, but a reconstruction. Pappas's job was to make the auditorium, seemingly sprung from mirage, reappear. The strings and winds and baritones missed no note, nor lieder.

Claudia L'Engle Adams, singer and pianist, founded the Ladies' Friday Musicale in her downtown home in 1890 and died there on East Monroe Street five years later, twenty-nine years old. Newspapers listed no cause.

A short *History of the Ladies' Friday Musicale* published around 1906 calls Claudia L'Engle Adams "a musician of great ability and rare musical feeling, who had fine musical training at the Peabody Conservatory of Music, Baltimore, Maryland."[5]

Before sunrise Sunday morning, March 26, 1995, antique settees and clocks, armchairs and archives, piano hammers and wind keys, original libretti and Stephen Foster swamp scores melted in the Friday Musicale's grand old hall at 645 Oak Street.[6]

The Ladies' Friday Musicale arose from the Women's Club Movement, which sought to bring *culture*, art being deemed women's business, to *community*. Wealthy white women, their education and talents otherwise untapped, tapped their husbands' bank accounts to push painting and sculpture and classical music and "appreciation" of literature and languages.

When Claudia L'Engle Adams died, "the members of the Ladies' Friday Musicale" officially "resolved," according to strictest business form and etiquette, "to express [their] deep sorrow [and] great esteem and admiration."

With yellow ribbons tied at the bottom and top of folded powder-blue cards, "the ladies" stated, "She it was who brought us together, and her's [*sic*] the spirit that was ever the stimulus to our endeavors."

From the height of the hopping '20s to the inception of the Great Depression, for four years, Concordia Hall had stood empty. The Musicale bought the large wooden gymnasium of the short-lived private girls' Concordia School in 1929, a decade after the school opened.

In March 1995 Margaret Fleet, president of the Friday Musicale, stood in the charred wastes and declared the oldest musical organization in Florida could not be deterred by the fact of a random arsonist torching its structures.

That Monday morning, the day after arson, the Florida *Times-Union's* Steve Patterson wrote of three fires started at the Riverside/Brooklyn line within a half hour. One fire caused a half million dollars' worth of damage at Blue Cross Blue Shield's health insurance offices at 320 Riverside Avenue. Another scorched the back of a Victorian gingerbread house at 630 May Street. The largest of the fires reduced the Friday Musicale to cinders.[7]

Firefighters received the call at 5:20 a.m., found the May Street house burning, and took the Blue Cross call at 5:39. These fires were the latest in more than fifty Riverside arsons since January 1993.

In July 1995 the Associated Press reported a task force investigating seventeen fires "in the downtown and nearby Riverside areas."[8] A thirty-five-year-old man, Calvin Joppy, was arrested in March 1994, running from a triangle of fires at three downtown law firms, carrying a dagger and a lighter. One month later, Assistant State Attorney Ginnifer Gee dropped charges due to lack of evidence. Joppy was arrested again for two more downtown arsons in July 1995.[9]

On February 27, 1996, Jim Schoettler's story in *the Florida Times-Union* began, "The fires kept burning, one after another."[10]

Pappas investigated every contour of the original building. By 1998 the new auditorium rose in the ghostly outline of the old, its rows of glass chandeliers, intricately grained floors of oak, and stage curtains of rich plush velvet taking shape in the shape of the lost. The greatest difference between the new Musicale and the old was the cement block construction finished with stucco, versus the original brick façade on wood frame. Astonishingly, patrons who'd attended shows at the Friday Musicale for decades said they couldn't tell the difference.

## 7. Old St. Andrews Church

Old St. Andrews Episcopal Church, Ted says, was collapsing. "Even today," Ted says, "the tower still leans." As the church, built in 1887, settled over time, the tower, with its louvered belfry, began to pitch slightly, and when Pappas restored the church in 1997, funds didn't exist to correct it.

Pappas replaced the roof and several large ceiling pieces, stained-glass windows, the floor, numerous pews, and old wood in the tower. Rain came straight into the nave through the holes in the roof; so did pigeons, and Mark remembers homeless people seeking shelter in the abandoned church.

Pappas added a kitchen off one side of the transept and a covered walkway leading to bathrooms and office/storage space on the other side.

Fernandina Beach architect Robert Schuyler designed the church in 1887, the year before Jacksonville's largest Yellow Fever epidemic, and its original members saw the Gothic Revival structure as a new beacon of hope. It survived the Great Fire of 1901, the third largest urban conflagration in American history, standing just east of the fire's periphery. The fire decimated almost all of Downtown of what was, at the time, the city of Jacksonville.

The 1889 edition of *King's Handbook of Notable Episcopal Churches in the United States* called St. Andrews "one of the most satisfying pieces of architecture in the South," adding, "It is built of pressed brick laid in black mortar, the trimmings being of stone. The ground plan is cruciform, the vestry-room on one side and the organ-chamber on the other forming the transepts. The chancel and nave are separated by three arches of masonry. The chancel, in addition to the usual furniture, has seats for a vested choir of 40 voices. The interior woodwork of the building is Florida pine, carefully selected and as carefully put together. The doors, a special gift, are made of solid mahogany. The ceiling is paneled with yellow pine. The tower rises to a height of 120 feet, and is the highest now in the city."[11]

When the congregation moved to Arlington in 1957, it left its original structure behind to deteriorate. Four decades later, enough preservationists and civic leaders had banded together to finance

Old St. Andrews Church, 1998, courtesy Ted Pappas

the structure's salvation for its new role as auditorium for the Jacksonville Historical Society.

On the day Ted, Mark, and I walk through the old wooden structure, it stands empty, a wedding planned for the weekend. In fact, in 1999 Mark Pappas was one of the first to get married in the newly restored church.

Pointing to the ceiling, Ted says, "You can see there's kind of a herringbone up there. The trusses were collapsing. We had to replace those large steel plates and bolts in between and rebuild a lot of the trusses."

When he began restoration, the glass was falling out of the windows. At some point, church administration had begun replacing the original stained-glass windows with tinted glass. Even now, Ted feels disappointed that the quality of some of the stained-glass replacement doesn't equal that of the others. The first stained-glass work he commissioned "was very intricate and the colors quite subtle," he says, but in order to have the windows finished in time for the grand opening, later window replacements were rushed.

For Mark, Old St. Andrews has sentimental value not only because he was married here, but because the church was one of his first projects after coming to work for his father. "He did with me what he did with my sisters, Christy and Mary," Mark says. "He put me at the front desk answering phones and dealing with everybody coming in. Back then, there was so much going and everything hadn't been digitized yet. It was the best way to learn what was happening, who's who and what's what, the best way to learn the business. I was never a good salesperson, but I did some marketing. At a small firm, you do a lot. I started project management with St. Andrews."

As always, Ted Pappas's career, artistry, and family life intersected. He brought his children in to work with the firm, just as he'd first opened his office in his Uncle John and Aunt Alexandra's historic retail and apartment building.

## 8. *The Historic Moves into the Future*

Attorney Doug Milne and Ted Pappas have been close friends for more than fifty years. They worked together in saving Duval High School, the Seminole Club, and other historic structures, partnered on the Milne-Pappas Building, perhaps Ted Pappas's *magnum opus*, even restored and rented out an 1870 hotel building now called River House Apartments in Riverside.

Doug likens Ted's ability in working equally well on contemporary designs and historic structures to "the athlete who can play quarterback for the football team, pitch for the baseball team and score three-pointers on the basketball court."

Says Doug, "There are a few people you meet in life who are just so smart you realize you're wasting your time second-guessing them. Ted's that way. He's very meticulous, but he's also both responsive and creative. And with the experience he's had in all these different areas, you just stand back and let him do his thing."

Two of the traits of that intelligence, Doug says, are Ted's curiosity and constant inspiration, and they form a kind of feedback loop. The two friends have a longtime habit of attending seminars and conferences together.

"He never goes anywhere without a notepad and a pencil," Doug says. "He takes copious notes, asks lots of questions, gets the names of lots of books and then he reads them. He's interested in everything and wants to know about everything."

In fifty years, Doug Milne predicts, "Ted Pappas will be remembered as a person people should have listened to more and paid more attention to in terms of vision for the city." Few people have as strong an understanding both of how the city should preserve and use its historic architecture and how it should move into the future. The best illustration of Ted's ability to work with the historic and create something new, Doug says, was the office at 100 Riverside Avenue, now remembered as the Milne-Pappas Building.[12]

Notes to Chapter Nine

1. Charles Pillans III (attorney), in discussion with the author, May 2018.

2. Peter Behringer (entrepreneur), in discussion with the author, June 2014.

3. Doug Milne (attorney and friend), in discussion with the author, May 2021.

4. Sandy Strickland, "Duval High School, Old No. 1, Has Outlived Its Students," *Florida Times-Union* (Jacksonville, FL), February 11, 2018.

5. Isabelle S. Perry, "History of the Ladies' Friday Musicale," (private collection of Friday Musicale), 1906.

6. "15 Arsons in City Spur Probe by Task Force," *Miami Herald* (Miami, FL), July 8, 1995.

7. Associated Press, "Jacksonville Arsons Burn 15 Buildings in Past 10 Months," *Orlando Sentinel*, July 7, 1995.

8. Associated Press, "Jacksonville Arsons," *Orlando Sentinel*, July 7, 1995.

9. "Felon Accused of Arson," *Tampa Tribune* (Tampa, FL), July 17, 1995.

10. Jim Schoettler, "Arson Task Force Sees Arrests Rise," *Florida Times-Union* (Jacksonville, FL), February 27, 1996.

11. Jacksonville Historic Landmarks Commission, *Jacksonville's Architectural Heritage* (Gainesville: University Press of Florida, 1989), 223.

12. Doug Milne (attorney, friend), in discussion with the author, May 2021.

# Ten

## The Milne-Pappas Building, 100 Riverside Avenue

### 1. *Architectural Home and Self-Portrait*

The fisheye lens best captured the curves of the landing and stairs. The lens bends the blond wood of walls and the windows inward. The image reminds me of an Anthony Burgess essay from the 1980s, riffing off the title of the Marilyn Monroe musical comedy, *But Do Blondes Prefer Gentlemen?* Now I'm in danger of mixing up my references, because I also think of the historic H.C. Hare Co. Building, which Ted Pappas customized into his own offices as a kind of self-portrait, and I'm thinking of the great 1974 John Ashberry poem named for the 1524 Parmigianino painting, *Self-Portrait in a Convex Mirror.*

Those confusions come together in the photograph of Ted Pappas standing before those very stairs and curved blond cypress landings for a December 1980 *Florida Times-Union* story. He looks down at the camera from left of center, great drapes of houseplant tendrils hanging from exposed rafters down the corridor to the other side.

Attorney and longtime friend, Doug Milne, still remembers the day he and Ted first walked into the abandoned building. "There was a sign on it, so we called the broker. He let us in. Now this was a two story building and Ted immediately envisions how he can make it a three story building without altering the exterior." With front windows twenty feet high, Ted told Doug how they could add a second and third level that "floated," the floors not reaching all the way to the walls.[1]

After Ted's long tenure at his uncle's building on Washington Street, he'd found the perfect exoskeleton of an historic building. Its interior was his to redesign and repurpose to create his artistic home. *Florida Architect* Magazine featured the Pappas Building in its Fall 1980 issue. The jury who'd given it an award for "Excellence in Architecture" praised its "clarity in execution," and called it "a strong concept, a building within a building."[2]

That phrase could hardly be more *apropos* for Ted Pappas. As each of his designs began within and "worked itself out"—literally by working outward, each was a "building within a building." Moreover, that phrase fit Ted's double focus, looking to the old and creating anew.[3]

Milne-Pappas Building, 1980, courtesy Ted Pappas

Milne-Pappas Building, 1980, courtesy Ted Pappas

The Milne-Pappas Building epitomized that principle. It resurrected a handsome but aesthetically modest building, barely "historic" (especially by standards elsewhere) as it dated only to 1940 and made the interior entirely new.

Beside a photo of a middle-aged Ted Pappas, thick piping in primary colors behind him, wearing a white polo shirt, leaning his dark and hirsute arms across blueprints, and looking daringly at the camera, ran a quotation from Ted about "the challenge" being "twofold." Obviously the "economic equation" had to work, but he also hoped "to give the building" a "spiritual uplift."

He said, "This structure gave me a great opportunity to do that by dealing with spaces, voids and color in a rather dramatic way. The real challenge was to demonstrate that doing contemporary things to old buildings does more than just restore them. It makes them relevant for contemporary society."

Ted Pappas, photo by William A. Greer, *Florida Architect* Magazine,
Fall 1980

Though preservationists would not have called this redesign a
restoration, the Hare Building proved perfectly suited for Ted's
artistic vision. It was handsome, old, distinguished, yet still basically
a marmoreal cut stone box. Its conversion into the Milne-Pappas

Building maintained its outward shape and brought it a new inner spirit, a new "spiritual" vitality.[4]

Later, seeking landmark status for the building, Ted wrote Thomas Purcell, chair of the Jacksonville Historic Preservation Commission, "Constructed of brick and ornamental cut stone, the building was designed by Clyde L. Harris with Mellen C. Greeley serving as consulting architect. A 1949 addition was also designed by Clyde L. Harris. The 1896 date over the doorway refers to the founding of the H.C. Hare Company."[5] Three years after Hare left in 1963, a vocational school, Florida Technical College, moved in. When Pappas and partner Doug Milne purchased the building in 1979, it had stood vacant for years.

Pappas always worked from the inside out. On wilder and more natural sites, in the mountains or at the beach, the outer wilderness came in. At the Milne-Pappas Building, city center, the stone exterior yielded interior soft yellow cypress and houseplants in corners and corridors. Photos of the front lobby show houseplants, exposed pipes, internal porthole windows, blinds, architectural castoffs like corbels from older historic structures, and dark plush carpets.

As in his residential designs and in the interior redesigns of the Doty Building on Washington Street, you could stand on upper floors, stair landings, or mezzanines, and look down into lower floors and from there to the outside. The building opened from a kernel within and spun upward and outward. You looked from a curved upper landing across vertical striations in the wood down layers of windows and hanging plants.

Down linear walkways alongside drawing stations, dark ochre and red carpets bled up into soft lights around tall, thin, dark green potted plants to upper light dispersed along dark exposed girders and red pipes running beneath light wooden rafters.

From outside at night, the contrasts of old and new, of exterior and interior, worked a strange magic. The strong white stone façade broke only in three tall rectangular windows and the windowed doorway, each topped by thin horizontal bars of glass, all fenestration puncturing the exterior stone with tempting views of soft light on amber interior scenes. The effect was spellbinding, a secret view into soft warm nurturing light in the hard contrast of urban night.

## 2. *"Haskell's Highway"*

Then along came Haskell's Highway. On June 30, 1993, the *Florida Times-Union* reported on "three buildings with varied backgrounds […] proposed for protection under city ordinances." Beth Reese Cravey described the history and cultural significance of the 1914 Maceo Elks Lodge Building in LaVilla, the 1949 Murray Hill Theatre, and the H.C. Hare Co. Building "in the way of the planned widening of Riverside Avenue." Cravey gave least attention to the Hare Co./Milne-Pappas Building, the latter now "threatened by the state Department of Transportation's plan to eventually widen Riverside Avenue to six lanes."[6]

Beverly Keneagy's story of March 6 served it better. Its lede ran, "Architect Ted Pappas estimates that half of Jacksonville's downtown buildings have been bulldozed in the name of progress." Keneagy continued, "He doesn't want the same thing to happen to his office building—just so a road can come through."[7]

Clyde Harris was still alive, in his nineties, and threatening a design so recently given new life by younger vision seemed an awful way to treat an old architect. Meanwhile, Pappas said, "We've lost half of downtown because people have bulldozed fine old buildings." The story quoted Ted making sadly necessary and obvious statements like, "Anytime you put an interstate highway through a neighborhood, it ruins it."

That neighborhood was Brooklyn, between Riverside and LaVilla, and its destruction has continued unabated. Platted just after the Civil War by a Confederate veteran named Miles Price who sold lots to former slaves and United States Colored Troops

Milne-Pappas Building, 1980, courtesy Ted Pappas

veterans, Brooklyn remained a historically black neighborhood until recently. Since the year 2000, five-over-one style apartment buildings have replaced block after block of historic Brooklyn. The style takes its name from the legalization of increased flooring built entirely of wood, frequently resulting in five floors of cheap wood frame construction built atop a single floor of concrete platform.

Reggie Bridges, once known as Brooklyn's unofficial historian, lost his house the summer of 2019 when Vestcor Companies demolished it to build a five-over-one complex called The Lofts at Brooklyn. A banner stretched across a construction fence where Reggie's house once stood and promised "urban living" coming soon. To bring "urban living" to Brooklyn, bulldozers demolished Reggie Bridges's house and the homes of his neighbors. Most of them, including Reggie, accepted the small payout and moved. Reggie had lived there for fifty-six years.[8]

Milne-Pappas Building, 1980, courtesy Ted Pappas

The dismantling and demolition of Brooklyn had begun years earlier. On March 25, 1997, *Folio Weekly* headlined a story, "Construction Mogul Extols the Virtues of a $22 Million Riverside Ave. Widening," above which ran a photo of Ted Pappas and the question, "Haskell's Highway?" *Folio* pointed out that the expansion would bring Riverside Avenue closer to "the offices of one of the city's wealthiest and most influential businessmen—construction mogul Preston Haskell." Yet, "while Haskell has been the project's most outspoken proponent, he insists the widening is being done to benefit thousands of downtown commuters."

Buildings on the west side of Riverside Avenue, however, stood in the way and taxpayers would pay $17.6 million to purchase and remove them.

"The building at 100 Riverside Avenue," *Folio* said, "is one of the project's speed bumps. For 17 years, it has been home to Pappas

Associates, Architects. When Ted Pappas bought the building, it was abandoned and desperately in need of repair." After "transforming it into a showpiece," Pappas and his building were "preparing for the seemingly inevitable sacrifice."

Asked about the fate of the Pappas Building, Haskell said, "This isn't one person's project or one property's project. This is a project for the whole of Riverside."[9]

It wasn't. It was a widening of a corridor between interstate exit ramps and Downtown at the expense of Brooklyn, several historic Riverside Avenue structures, and architect Ted Pappas's masterwork of simultaneous forward-facing art and historic preservation.

### 3. *Heart and Headquarters as Debris*

Ted fought the loss of his artistic home and headquarters for a decade. On April 6, 2002, the *Florida Times-Union's* David Bauerlein wrote, "The state Department of Transportation's long and costly march to clear the way for a wider Riverside Avenue took another stride this week with the demolition of Jacksonville architect Ted Pappas's former office."

The Pappas family stood on the opposite corner and watched bulldozers demolish it. Mary Lee wept, while Ted kept an arm around her and watched, his mouth set into his face reserved and stoic like a heartbroken smile. Heavy metal claws smashed through the very spot in the building where his personal office stood.

"It was done so quickly," Ted said, "and all your experiences run through your mind, so many wonderful experiences, and just seeing the environment for those experiences demolished in a matter of minutes," oh, "it was devastating."

At one point, as the Pappas family watched, the interior of the building opened up wide in the lights of the night. It was an irony. Ted always said the interior determined the exterior. That was the creative impetus. Now the opposite crashed in, and demolition machinery ripped open the interior and exposed to the night that sensuously curved blond cypress stairway.

That stairway had always been central. Showcase in the fisheye lens. The curved, soft hardwood of the building within a building of rectangular stone. The place, Bauerlein wrote, "where Pappas's son, Mark, first met his future wife, Jennifer, when she was working as Pappas's assistant. Within minutes, the staircase was gone too, joining the growing pile of debris."[10]

## 4. *Where/Here There is No Vision*

Artist Steve Williams has known Ted Pappas for more than thirty years. In fact, he took Ted's daughter Christy to the prom in high school. "The Pappases are the nicest people on earth," he says. "And Mary Lee is the loveliest human being I've ever met."

He loves Ted's designs, calls the Singleton Senior Center his favorite, and says he misses the Milne-Pappas Building terribly. "Just the other day, I was thinking about that building and just how stupid it is that a building that beautiful could ever be torn down. And just to widen a road!" He describes the building as "beautifully classic on the *out*side, so modern *in*side. It felt like something you'd see in Manhattan. It was like Halston or somebody was gonna be in the back room."

Steve started working with Ted when his father, Roger Williams, who owned Harbinger Signs, sent him over to work out signage deals for Pappas buildings. He remembers Ted always having new ideas about Downtown or having some kind of philosophical insight Steve thought he should write down.

Perhaps what's astounded Steve most about Ted, however, is the way he's stayed inspired through the years. Steve refers to riverfront greenspace plans and ideas to create a central green corridor linked to James Weldon Johnson Park in the very center.

"One of the things we've missed as a city these last 50 years is not listening to Ted Pappas more," Steve says. "We missed out on his vision, even when he offered it to us for free." Yet after seeing the Milne-Pappas Building demolished, Ted's inspiration continued. Steve says he couldn't comprehend it but considers such inspiration the energy that fuels a visionary.

His memory makes a quick detour, and he laughs. He had an art studio in an old warehouse a block or more down the street from the Milne-Pappas. In the back of that building was an old recording studio. Lynyrd Skynyrd used to record back there.[11]

Mary Acree, Ted's oldest daughter, remembers the studio, too. "I was talking to my dad about it the other day," she says. "He would walk me down to it. I was just in middle school. We'd hear .38 Special playing in there. I think that's who it was."[12]

"It was Molly Hatchet," Mark says. "At least, that's what I've always remembered and told people. Anyway, Hatchet is much cooler than .38 Special."[13]

Whoever it was, Mary says her dad doesn't remember the band at all. Steve says the building was full of dilapidated 1970s recording equipment from the days when Jacksonville's Southern Rock bands called it Riverside Studios. When the Department of Transportation demolished that side of Riverside Avenue, all that old equipment went to the landfill.

Riverside Studios brings Steve, Mary, and Mark a moment of bemusement, but losing the Milne-Pappas Building slashed a wound that still hasn't healed. For a long time, Mary says, it hurt to see new development rise where her father's building once stood. She's better now. She had lunch with her daughter there earlier on this particular day that she speaks with me.

Every now and then, instead of referring to "100 Riverside Avenue," what Ted called what others dubbed the Pappas Building, Ted will just say, "Where BurgerFi is now," referring to the corporate fast-food chain. Surely that euphemism for an absence, a loss, a tragedy says more than he means it to say.

What Steve Williams says about the vision Ted Pappas offered his hometown reminds me, appropriately oddly, of a sermon I heard in church when I was young. The preacher spoke anecdotally of a church that quoted a Bible verse, Proverbs 29:18, on its sign: "Where there is no vision, the people perish." Yet in the cautionary tale expounded in this sermon, the 'W' stencil had fallen. Inadvertently the congregation announced, "Here, there is no vision. The people perish."

## 5. *Exofrenikós; or Honoring the Brick*

So I'm thinking about the distinction between a design and the structure that embodies it. It's something of a platonic question—the difference between the idea and its realization. Every architectural retrospective includes designs never built and those designs are no less real. On the other hand, I've seen again and again how what's happened to the designs Ted's executed, whether through insensitive remodeling or demolition, causes him pain.

Yet built into Ted's understanding of being an architect is compromise. He frequently refers to Frank Lloyd Wright's distinction of the architect, as against the painter and poet, as creative interpreter. The architect is given a charge and specification, marked with a budget, and ordered to make a final place of a space.

"It makes an architect different from an artist who paints or a writer who writes," Ted tells me, "not necessarily constrained by clients or demands or tastes, someone who does their own thing and it comes out of their own soul. They're not doing something subject to critique in the same way, something that a party who's hiring you can dictate."

Then again, we're discussing Frank Lloyd Wright, as egocentric an architect and artist as his native land, of which he was so fond of claiming dictated his work. So, what made the difference? "For

Wright," Ted says, "it was his personality, but also for sure, he had such gifts. Wright was eccentric, he was talented, he knew it, and he had clients ready to put their money behind his ideas."

When Ted's designed car dealerships, Audi and Hyundai, for Jack Hanania, he's forced to work from a template. The work of which he's most proud is for clients willing "to put their money behind his ideas." He was his own such client at the Hare Co./ Milne-Pappas Building.

We discuss the strangeness and mental instability stereotypical of artists as against that of the general population. I argue that not only do those stereotypes, often romanticized, hurt the artist, but that the American public at large struggles with as many addictions, depressions, and manias as the artist. "Like writers and painters, I think," Ted says, "well, let me back up. My mother used to say that architects were exofrenic [exofrenikós/εξωφρενικός], which means 'outside your mind.'"

"She meant that people who grew up to be artists, and she knew other young Greeks in the neighborhood who grew up to be artists, in order to be creative, were not conventional. If you're an artist, you're different from conventionally thinking people."

Ted's daughters don't use the word "exofrenic," but they both assert, unprompted, how differently he thinks. In fact, instead of "outside your mind," Christy says he's "inside his own head all the time." Lovingly, Christy calls Ted "the most devoted family man," an "airhead," a "weirdo" and a "teddy bear," all in two sentences.

"He's always losing his car keys," Christy says. "But he's not really scatterbrained and airheaded, it's just where he's tuned in. He's both inside his own head and paying attention to the details of the world in a way most people aren't able to do. He sees details and structures in nature and in architecture that most of us don't see."[14]

Ted and I talk about Mies van der Rohe and Le Corbusier, about Frank Lloyd Wright and Louis Kahn, about architecture's twentieth-century struggle against "imitation imitating imitation."

Ted talks about design starting from the inside, working itself outward, but also listening to its site. It reminds me of Kahn's famous description of his discourse with his material.

"Brick says to you, 'I like an arch.' And if you say to Brick, 'Look, arches are expensive and I can use a concrete lintel over you. What do you think of that, Brick?'" Then Brick repeats, "I like an arch." And Kahn says, "You honor the material. You can only do it if you honor the brick and glorify the brick instead of shortchanging it."

Notes to Chapter Ten

1.  Doug Milne (attorney, friend), in discussion with the author, May 2021.

2.  "100 Riverside Avenue, Jacksonville," *Florida Architect*, Fall 1980.

3.  "Award, Excellence in Architecture," *Florida Architect*, Fall 1980.

4.  "Award," *Florida Architect*.

5.  Ted Pappas, letter to Thomas Purcell (archives of Jacksonville Historic Preservation Commission).

6.  Beth Reese Cravey, "Lodge, Theater, Office Examined," *Florida Times-Union* (Jacksonville, FL), June 30, 1993.

7.  Beverly Keneagy, "Landmark Designation is Sought," *Florida Times-Union* (Jacksonville, FL), March 6, 1993.

8.  Tim Gilmore, "Last House Standing; Or, How 'Brooklyn' Killed Brooklyn," *JaxPsychoGeo.com*, January 31, 2020.

9.  "Haskell's Highway? Construction Mogul Extols the Virtues of a $22 Million Riverside Ave. Widening," *Folio Weekly*, March 25, 1997.

10. David Bauerlein, "Riverside Widening Racks Up Costs," *Florida Times-Union* (Jacksonville, FL), April 6, 2002.

11. Steve Williams (artist) in discussion with the author, May 2021.

12. Mary Pappas Acree (daughter) in discussion with the author, May 2021.

13. Mark Pappas (son) in discussion with the author, May 2021.

14. Christy Pappas Gillam (daughter), in discussion with the author, May 2021.

# Eleven

## Epping Forest and The Bolles School

### 1. *Epping Forest*

In 1927 Alfred and Jessie Ball duPont, two of the wealthiest people in Florida, hired the Jacksonville architectural firm Marsh and Saxelbye to design their Mediterranean Revival style mansion, centered on a three-story entryway and tower. The style, which features rough plaster walls, clay barrel tile roofs, grand arches, and courtyards, mushroomed across Florida during the land boom of the 1920s, which ended in the stock market crash and the Great Depression.

In 1984 Raymond Mason, president of an oil, insurance, and communications conglomerate called The Charter Company, sold Epping Forest to Herb Peyton of Gate Petroleum, who decided to turn the residence into a yacht club and hired Ted Pappas for the job.

Alfred duPont was born into a family who made its wealth, through E. I. duPont de Nemours and Co., from explosives. The company would later become famous for its motto, "Better Things for Better Living…Through Chemistry," adopted in 1935, the year of Alfred's death, its manufacturing of Teflon, and some of the worst environmental crimes in American history, chronicled in attorney Robert Bilott's, 2019 book, *Exposure,* and the 2019 film,

*Dark Waters*, starring Mark Ruffalo as Bilott, the attorney who fights DuPont for environmental justice for decades.

But Alfred duPont went his own way. In 1920, after he left the family business and his first wife died, duPont married Jessie Ball, and Florida's runaway banking and real estate economy drew the couple south from Delaware. They bought controlling interests in Florida banks and decided to build their home at Christopher Point, just outside the then-new and Mediterranean Revival influenced neighborhoods of San Marco and San Jose.

Indeed, the duPonts built beside the new San Jose Hotel, also "Mediterranean," and one of the grandest new hotels in Florida. A similar hotel, the Vanderbilt, was supposed to have been built on the spot the duPonts chose. Half a century later, Ted Pappas would land some of his firm's most prestigious jobs at Epping Forest and at the Bolles School, which centered on the old San Jose Hotel, now called Bolles Hall. Pappas would be campus architect at Bolles for more than a decade.[1]

Alfred duPont had lived at Epping Forest for eight years when he died in 1935. His several infusions of his own wealth in Florida banks during the Depression stemmed banking panics. Even heading into the Depression, the duPonts kept opening banks across the state. In 1931 duPont told a friend on the Virginia Supreme Court, "Let this Depression pass, and it will surely pass. They all pass." His politics were decidedly with President Herbert Hoover and against the policies of Franklin Delano Roosevelt. He still maintained, "There is no power on earth that can stop the growth of Florida. It's the nation's last frontier."[2]

Jessie continued to live at Epping Forest, which she referred to as "the shack," until her own death in 1970. Her politics shifted left of her husband's, supporting Roosevelt's New Deal.[3] Yet, though she focused her wealth increasingly on charities, she ended contributions to educational institutions when she found out they admitted black students.[4] Today, the charitable foundation that operates in Jessie Ball duPont's name focuses on diversity, inclusiveness and equality.

Her brother, banker and financier Ed Ball, sold Epping Forrest in 1972 to Raymond Mason, who, four years later, hosted a conference at Epping Forest with President Gerald Ford and Egyptian President Anwar Sadat, conducted by Secretary of State Henry Kissinger.[5]

In renovating and repurposing Epping Forest, Pappas also designed the new yacht club's fitness center, walkway, and swimming pool, in keeping with the original stucco walls and red clay tile roof, as well as the gatehouse, which shares architectural idioms like lions' heads with the mansion.

But the biggest challenges Pappas faced in the renovation were increasing dining capacity and installing central air-conditioning. Upstairs, he converted the master bedroom into a ballroom and created a grand staircase off its side, but those moves were easy compared to the difficulties of what's usually a simple enterprise.

"You want to put air conditioning in an old building, of course," Ted says, "and most people would just drop the ceiling and put the a/c behind it. But we couldn't do that." San Jose Country Club across the street had done just that, but Pappas found the idea unconscionable.

By way of explanation, he points at the magnificent coffered ceiling with its massive oak beams and intricately hand-painted stenciling in floral patterns, arabesques, and winding serpents. Capital brackets show Green Man motifs. It would be a crime to cover such artwork and a piece of the house's architectural value as intrinsic as the multicolored staggered tiles between brick tiles in the floor. So, Pappas designed a series of cabinets, some now fronted with wine racks, to nestle unnoticed against the walls and hold the air-conditioning.

In the original dining room, heavy masculine woodwork in the doors, chairs, display cabinet, and sideboard offsets the cream of the stucco. The central table seats eight chairs. The dining room was large for a private residence in its time, but it wouldn't accommodate a yacht club. So Pappas designed extra dining room space out back and moved the terrace and surrounding balustrade toward the river.

The new dining room begins from the original dining room and rear wall of the house and stands on the original terrace space. The line to which the dining room extends is about where the stone balustrade once stood. Inside the addition, barrel vaults extend toward the river and end in arched windows that punctuate a wall of glass with a thin steel framework painted a dark green.

Walking along the back terrace, Ted points to how the terrace was extended beneath the magnificent ancient oaks. For an historic addition and repurposing to work, Mark says, you have to be able to tell the addition is new, but also how it respects the original design.

We walk beneath the rear wrought-iron balcony with its three central windows pointed with ogee arches. The exterior wall features plaster pelicans and capitals with acanthus leaves centered on strange gaunt vampiric faces. Coming around the side of the former master bedroom, which Ted converted to a banquet room, we stop before a grand staircase with multiple turns of stairs and landings.

"With the residence becoming a yacht club," Ted says, "Peyton wanted to have weddings here, and we designed this staircase with the specific intention of showcasing the bride coming down the stairs." That's really the whole purpose of the staircase, made of precast concrete with a pinkish hue and surrounded by red and purple ginger plants. Most local wedding photographers know this staircase. The balusters mimic those of the balustrade.

Since the drop from the banquet room is steep, the stairs descend from the balcony, then fork into twin sections from the first landing and descend to lower landings. The steps that lead to the ground cut back in the opposite direction and meet before a central arch.

Epping Forest, cover of *Florida Architect* Magazine, November–
December 1989

Through the arch of the grand stairway, the door opens into the
bar. Noticeably, thirty-five years after the renovation, the massive
oak beams, with their colorful floral and serpentine stenciling,

have started to split. Ironically, the splitting comes both from age and, Ted says, from how central air conditioning dries out the air.

We climb the interior stairs of the central tower at the front of the house, rising from the old sitting room, the intimacy and human scale of which makes it Ted's favorite room in the house, past the midlevel, story-high Palladian window to the bedroom floor. Whatever intimacies and intricacies this level of the house originally contained are gone now. Ted did what he had to do, removing walls and anterooms to open the whole floor for event space. He doesn't love it like he does the ground floor.

Ted speaks of how larger histories obscure countless smaller ones, including how Marsh and Saxelbye, who also designed the San Jose Hotel, now Bolles Hall, and Ted's own house in historic Avondale, brought European craftsmen to work on these buildings. Builders and architects often bemoan the loss of the intricate trade and craft knowledge that went into these historic buildings, a sad fact that challenges preservationists in keeping old designs to original character and intent. William Mulford Marsh and Harold Saxelbye, who worked so frequently with Mediterranean Revival designs, employed a well-known group of Italian plasterers, six or eight men, who moved throughout Florida from one site to the next. Their names are lost to history, but their master craftsmanship remains across the state. Those plasterers worked for Marsh and Saxelbye on Epping Forest, the San Jose Hotel, and the house on Elizabeth Place that Ted has called home since the 1970s.

## 2. *The Bolles School*

Just down shore from the site where the Vanderbilt Hotel was to be built, and where the duPonts built Epping Forest in its stead, the San Jose Hotel rose on the bluff above the river where slave trader and cotton magnate, Zephaniah Kingsley, owned one of his smaller plantations. Marsh and Saxelbye sought to build the San Jose in the likeness of an "ancient Spanish castle." It took less than three years for one of the grandest hotels in Florida to go bankrupt.[6]

The Bolles School prides itself on being one of the most prestigious private schools in Florida, with strong academics and special regard for athletics. It operated as a military school until 1962 and first admitted female students in 1971. Throughout much of the 1980s and '90s, Ted Pappas was the school's primary architect, spearheading more than forty projects, ranging from the restoration of the original hotel building, now Bolles Hall, to the design of the Cindy and Jay Stein Fine Arts Building and Lynch Theater, most of the Whitehurst Lower School Campus, the Olympic-sized swimming pool and the school's football stadium.

Just how Bolles came to be, and how it grew into a primary and secondary school that costs five times the average tuition of a Florida public university, is a confusing and controversial story. The San Jose Hotel opened on January 1, 1926, and Agnes Cain

Bolles School, late 1980s, courtesy Ted Pappas

Painter, longtime secretary to deceased real estate tycoon Richard J. "Dicky" Bolles, held the first mortgage. In 1927 she took out a mortgage for the hotel's furnishings. In 1928 she filed for foreclosure and bought the hotel outright.

Cain formed a corporation called the Bolles Investment Company. She elected herself president, and her husband, twenty-seven years her junior, secretary. Then she sold the hotel and its furnishings to the investment company she'd just formed. She issued shares to herself and the Richard J. Bolles Estate, then leased the property to the Florida Military Academy. And so, the San Jose Hotel first became an educational institution.

Agnes and Roger Painter received the military school's rent and lived on the property, walking at will between the arches of the arcades and staring from the rare heights of a St. Johns River shoreline. They dallied in the lobbies with their rich dark masculine oak and pecky cypress, beneath the ornate corner towers with their high clay arches beneath red roofs. Through the long walkways, they watched the sun play on the flickering shards of the river. Not all tourist rooms had been converted to classrooms, and the Painters could trace with their fingertips hearts skewered with arrows carved by hand in high windowsills. When they desired, they could stand in the colonnaded peaks of the four-story towers on either side of the front central courtyard.

In the summer of 1932, the Painters gave the Florida Military Academy notice of eviction and opened their own school the following year named for their former boss. Agnes Cain had first met Roger Painter when Richard Bolles hired him as an office boy. When the couple married in 1923, Agnes was forty-eight years old, and Roger was twenty-one. In 1933 they founded the Bolles School.[7]

While the renovation and yacht club conversion of Epping Forest was one of the most prestigious projects of Pappas's career, his decade-and-a-half of continuous work at the Bolles School represented one of his most prominent long-lasting business relationships. Crossing Bolles with Ted and Mark Pappas is like touring the trajectory of his architectural thinking across those years.

When Bolles added a lower school in 1983, with pre-Kindergarten through fifth grade, Ted designed most of the buildings of the Whitehurst Campus (really a part of the main Bolles Campus), countering the scale of Bolles Hall, which housed upper school classes, and its grandiosity with a series of small, spare, and minimalist buildings that create the effect of a small village. If it takes a village to raise a child, Bolles's youngest students seem to matriculate in one.

Ted says, "We designed the prototype building in the manner of Frank Lloyd Wright, where we destroyed the box by opening up the corners, and built the other lower school buildings similarly." Indeed, the corners open into windows and porches, while wide eaves reach into the sheltering shade of close stands of oak trees.

We walk through Bolles Hall, the old San Jose Hotel itself, built by six hundred workers in six months in 1926: one hundred twenty-five hotel rooms, opening night described by *The Florida Times-Union* as a "brilliant gathering" as "unto the courts of Spain with all of its splendor."[8] Ted points to the administrative offices, which his firm designed, and speaks of refitting the cafeteria. The firm worked on various Bolles Hall renovations from 1987 to 1995. The halls are dark and masculine, heavy with massive oak and coffered ceilings. Mark, who was a student here himself in the late 1980s, recalls construction being staggered against class schedules, much of it completed in summer months.

In the grand courtyard, Mark points to the English and Social Studies departments, international boarders from India, Saudi Arabia, and Northern Europe residing on the third floor. On the other side of the palatial old building, we walk the arcade toward the river. On the mosaic tile walkway, between stuccoed arches, beneath dark wooden beams and joists, the sunlight dancing lambent on ten thousand ripples in the river seems the ultimate visual terminus.

Mark cuts back and forth between reminiscing and explaining the business. He shows me the rooms where he took classes from his favorite teachers. He recalls seeing fighter planes from Naval Air Station Jacksonville soar over the river in the last years of the Cold War, reading Jacksonville-based novelist Pat Frank's 1959 apocalyptic novel *Alas, Babylon!*, and joking with friends about how well positioned they would be, in a town with three major military bases, if the Soviets rained down nuclear war. He's always been an optimist, he says, and laughs. Jacksonville would be wiped off the face of the earth. None of Mark's friends would have to trudge through toxic sludge with nuclear mutants and post-apocalyptic ghouls.

A few minutes later Mark's talking about how projects of various sizes kept the firm in strong standing with the school. "Sometimes you worked on dinky projects, which Dad always called 'churn work,'" Mark says. "By the time you got through the bureaucracy and everything else, you probably ended up losing money." Those jobs, however, were the links between big projects like a new arts center and a new football stadium. Meanwhile, other architects took other campus jobs, but you kept bidding and designing and working. Certainly, the Pappases never planned that so much of the campus would end up having been their work, but that's how the relationship aggregated and evolved.

At the Cindy and Jay Stein Fine Arts Building, Ted speaks of trying to do two things at once, different goals but complementary. He wanted "to break up the monotony," grand and lovely as it was, of the Florida Land Boom's lingering Mediterranean Revival influence, but echo that influence in arches and arcades with cleaner lines in concrete.

As the Bolles School places so much emphasis on athletics, it's inevitable the school's main architect throughout the 1980s would design several of its most significant sporting facilities. That includes the school's football stadium and field, designed in 1983, and its Olympic-sized swimming pool, designed in '89.

A quick flip through old Pappas Associates records turns up forty-four different projects from 1981 to 1995. Ted's work at Bolles spans a central portion of his career, including significant historic preservation work and conscientious contemporary design. The "churn work," maintaining the relationship between architect and client between bigger jobs, included parking improvements, dining rooms, and the campus entrance. The Bolles work is a microcosm of the continuous hard work and brilliance, when opportunity called for and allowed it, of this architect's long and fruitful career.

It's one thing to focus on opportunities met with vision, but it's also necessary to understand the practicality of the business. "We did small work here all the time," Mark says. "A gatehouse, coaches' offices. Then you'd get a big contract like the stadium. No project itself was Hawaiian vacation money, but it was good work to have and certainly when we went after other work, we promoted the fact that we were the campus architectural firm for the Bolles School for much of two decades."

Tim Gilmore

Notes to Chapter Eleven

1.  Jacksonville Historic Landmarks Commission, *Jacksonville's Architectural Heritage* (Gainesville: University Press of Florida, 1989), 276-79.

2.  "Florida is Right to Honor Alfred I. duPont, *Tampa Bay Business Journal* (Tampa, FL), August 21, 2000.

3.  Harris Powers, "Her Name Spells Aid: The Story of Jessie Ball duPont," *Orlando Sentinel* (Orlando, FL), September 13, 1953.

4.  Joseph Constant, *No Turning Back: The Black Presence at Virginia Theological Seminary* (Alexandria: Virginia Theological Seminary Press, 2009), 40.

5.  United Press International, "Sadat, Ford Welcoming Mat Spread," *Tampa Tribune* (Tampa, FL), November 2, 1975.

6.  Jacksonville Historic Landmarks Commission, *Jacksonville's Architectural Heritage* (Gainesville: University Press of Florida, 1989), 276-79.

7.  "History of Bolles," bolles.org, accessed May 12, 2021, https://www.bolles.org/about-us/the-history-of-bolles.

8.  Jacksonville Historic Landmarks Commission, *Jacksonville's Architectural Heritage* (Gainesville: University Press of Florida, 1989), 276-79.

# Twelve

## Libraries and Educational Centers

When Ted Pappas designed the Beaches Branch Library in Neptune Beach, Florida, in 1983, he reached the culmination of his work in several kinds of library projects. At the same time, he continued to explore the organic unfoldings that began when he designed the Mom's Folly mountain house to unfurl like a leaf, and continued through his fluid 30°-60° grid at the Singleton Senior Center. In the case of the Beaches Library, Pappas explored his fascination with the Golden Ratio.

Pappas had worked on library designs by two of Jacksonville's most celebrated earlier architects. The first was Taylor Hardwick's Haydon Burns Library in Downtown Jacksonville. Built in 1965, the library, now the headquarters of the Jessie Ball duPont Center, which houses nineteen separate nonprofit organizations, is generally considered one of the architectural jewels of the city. Then, in 1983, Pappas restored the Jacksonville Free Public Library, built between 1903 and 1905 and designed by the city's most famous historic architect, Henry John Klutho. Built in the neoclassical style of many of the nearly three thousand library buildings funded by steel tycoon Andrew Carnegie between 1901 and 1919, rather than Klutho's later signature Prairie Style made Southern, the structure is the oldest library building in the city.

Pappas pursued his own architectural impulses first in the Regency Square Branch Library in 1972, then the Charles Webb

OLD CARNEGIE LIBRARY Post Construction
Photograph - OFFICES FOR BEDELL
DITTMAR, DE VAULT, PILLANS AND GENTRY

Jacksonville Free Public Library / Bedell Building, 1983, courtesy Ted
Pappas

Wesconnett Regional Library in 1974, and finally the Beaches
Branch Library in 1983.

In the Neptune Beach library, Pappas continued the architecture
of unfurlings, of openings-out, of blooming, in his exploration
of the Golden Ratio. The Golden Ratio, also called the Golden
Mean or the Golden Section, identified by the Greek letter Phi
($\Phi$), associates closely to the Fibonacci Sequence, named for a
thirteenth-century Italian mathematician, in which each number
is the sum of the two numbers preceding: 1, 1, 2, 3, 5, 8, 13, 21, 34,
55 and so on. If you graph out a series of squares, the side lengths of
which are successive Fibonacci numbers, then connect the opposite
corners with circular arcs, you approximate a Golden Spiral, the
growth factor of which is Phi ($\Phi$). French mathematician Jacques
Philippe Marie Binet created the formula showing how the ratio

of two consecutive Fibonacci numbers tends to the Golden Ratio as *n* increases.

Importantly for Pappas, the Golden Ratio and Fibonacci Sequence are found in uncountable natural forms, including the flowering of an artichoke, the arrangement of scales on a pinecone, the spirals of ram horns and gourd tendrils, and most obviously the Nautilus shell. The seventeenth-century German astronomer and mathematician Johannes Kepler noticed the leaf patterns of many trees align in Fibonacci patterns. From any particular leaf on a cherry tree or an elm, follow the spiral one, two, three, and five turns and you'll find leaves lined up with the first. In various species, this leaf will be the second, the third, the fifth, the eighth, or the thirteenth. Examples could go on, seemingly *ad infinitum*, as Theodore Andrea Cook's fascinating 1979 book, *The Curves of Life*, demonstrates.

In architecture, the Golden Section is central to many of the world's most famous buildings, from the Cathédrale Notre-Dame de Paris to the Parthenon. In the Beaches Branch Library, you can see it in the building's external façade. You walk it in the library's floorplan.

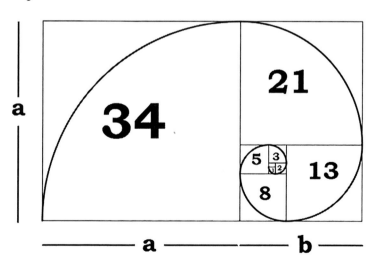

Golden Ratio, demonstrating Fibonacci Sequence

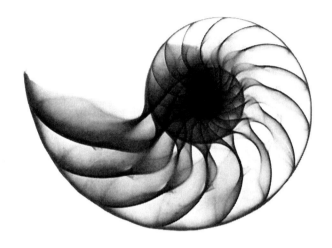

"X-Ray of Nautilus Shell" by Edward Charles Le Grice, ca. 1910

"The Ancient Greek buildings used the Golden Rectangle," Ted says. "On the Beaches Branch Library, the proportions of all the rectangles are Golden Sections." The center of each concrete panel in the façade features a horizontal staccato at a right angle to the fluting that bookmarks the sections on either side. "The fluting mimics that of columns on Ancient Greek temples," Ted says, "which adds movement and keeps them from looking so bulky." At the top of each staccato stands an antefix, which Pappas began using as the symbol for his architecture.

In Ancient Greek and Roman architecture, the antefix is a vertical block terminating and covering roof tiles. Frequently decorative, ancient antefixes featured the faces of mythological characters or a palmette motif or anthemion (ανθέμιον), with radiating petals. The floral motifs atop each staccato resemble palm fronds growing from a trunk or the opening of a flower.

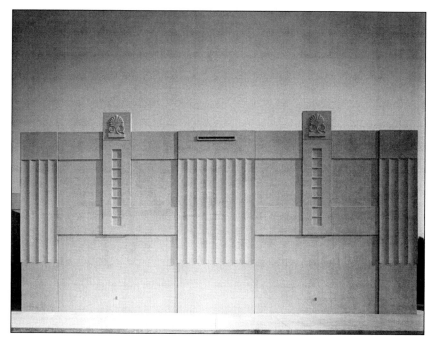

Beaches Branch Library, 1983, courtesy Ted Pappas

Ted's younger daughter, Christy Pappas Gillam, has fond memories of visiting the Beaches Library site with her father. "It seems like he was always working on a library," she says. She remembers many a Sunday afternoon when her father drove the kids around to whatever job he was working on. "He also liked stomping around in the dirt and walking the site. The library site became a playground for us."

Ted explained to his kids the Golden Ratio, even as he explained it all these years later to library staff on a walk-through. "I wish I had the eye he has," Christy says. "I think about the way he walks around the world and sees things in details the rest of us don't even pay attention to."[1]

Mark tells me a distinct influence on his father's architecture is a "love for the contemplative." For most of his life, Ted Pappas "has studied religion extensively," Mark says. "Not in a reductionist kind of way, but in an expansive way." While Ted's attended Greek

Webb Wesconnett Library, 1974, courtesy Ted Pappas

Orthodox services most of his life, he meets regularly with a Methodist church's Bible study group and has participated for the last five years in Sewanee, the University of the South's Education for Ministry program, which meets regionally at St. John's Episcopal Cathedral downtown. "Churches and libraries are some of his favorite projects," Mark says, "because they have the same needs for contemplation, for immersion."

That brings the question of what kind of atmosphere a library needs and how an architect seeks to create such an atmosphere. Ted says, "The building's interior determines its exterior and its primary purpose or function dictates the rest." In his design for the Charles Webb Wesconnett Regional Library, Ted included a plant-filled interior courtyard, open to sunlight and air, with community meeting rooms on either side. In the Beaches Branch, the Webb Wesconnett, and the Regency Square libraries, the reading room ceilings span overhead in a chessboard of light squares.

Webb Wesconnett Library, 1974, courtesy Ted Pappas

The entrance portico to Webb Wesconnett consists of a series of yellow brickwork arches, strangely both massive and light. Pappas chose a golden tan color for the brick, similar to what he'd used on St. John the Divine Greek Orthodox Church, similar again to a color he'd inherited from Harry Burns in his first residential commission. The brickwork looks earthen but sunlit, ancient but new.

Across the front of the library, four protruding arches connect each brick stanchion to the next. In between the arches score deep-cut radial lines, and the dentiling at the library's front corners leads to recessing of the sides. Together, these details give the front portico an added sense of dimension. So do reflections of the portico in windows. If you face a single brick stanchion, with its separate sets of arches rising to either side, the stanchion becomes a trunk, with arches radiating up and out like petals or fronds bursting in both directions.

*137*

Webb Wesconnett Library, 1974, courtesy Ted Pappas

You can also see a number of the themes and ideas Ted used in Webb Wesconnett in his Southeast Tape Company Building of 1989, in which he uses golden sand tones and stretches horizontals over rounded brick forms and fenestrated voids. The building is now the home of Daniel Memorial, founded in 1884, the oldest "child-serving agency" in Florida.

Pappas's design for the Regency Square Branch Library in 1972 was his first library design on his own after working on Hardwick's Haydon Burns Library in 1965. In contrast to other May Street School of Architecture designers like Robert Broward, who had worked with Frank Lloyd Wright and created his own clean streamlined style, Hardwick, Ted recalls, "liked to embellish. He was colorful." That adjective applies both to Hardwick's personality and to his work. Ted recalls Hardwick drove a gold Ford Thunderbird and that people referred to its hue as "Hardwick gold."

Working on the Haydon Burns Library, Ted learned that while he, himself, wanted to "destroy the box," Hardwick—and Ted means no disrespect, though their goals so differed—"liked to *decorate* the box." Both architects, Hardwick, older than most May Street architects, and Ted Pappas, just starting out, shared a love for the cantilever.

Ironically, Hardwick's Haydon Burns Library replaced the older Jacksonville Free Public Library, diagonally across the street, as the city's main downtown library. The first City Hall built after the Great Fire of 1901, also a Klutho design, this one heavily *Beaux-Arts* with a luxurious dome, the City demolished to give rise to Hardwick's new building.

When the movement toward historic preservation brought the oldest library to the attention of the oldest law firm in 1983, Ted Pappas was the architect to restore and resuscitate it. Working on the Carnegie library, Ted says, was a constant process of rediscovery. At times, historic preservation becomes a kind of architecture in reverse. Beginning with the ways the years have disrespected an original design, the restorative architect works backward until the original jewel shows forth, then decides how to make it practical for the present.

When Pappas designed the Regency Square Branch Library in 1972, he featured elements he'd give fuller expression in the Webb Wesconnett and Beaches Branch Libraries. Having worked on Taylor Hardwick's library design, Ted now had the chance to "destroy the box" of his own library.

He used the same chessboard lighting, hiding HVAC features alternately between light squares, that he'd later use at Webb Wesconnett. He incorporated plant life as an interior architectural element and built spacious arcades out front. He designed a concave wall of skintled brick as visual terminus from the front entrance, a partition, he told *Brick in Architecture* Magazine, "constructed of bricks projecting at differing degrees with random voids to excite the pattern."[2]

Regency Square Branch Library, 1972, courtesy Ted Pappas

Dramatic early photographs of the library show checkerboard squares with eXes across the flooring, angled bookshelves by front plate glass windows, and Mies van der Rohe's Barcelona chairs. Elsewhere, Le Corbusier lounge chairs stand at right angles before Eames-like card catalogue tables, and registration desks stand behind cedar beams and before curtained backdrops.

Sifting through old photos, negatives, and contact sheets, I find a young Ted Pappas pictured from above. He's sitting on the floor in the Regency Branch Library. He wears tennis shoes and perches his elbows on his knees. It's a momentary playfulness that Ted doesn't remember, staring up at us from almost fifty years ago.

No consideration of Ted Pappas's contemplative architecture, so often concerned with scholastic, religious, and library settings and structures, could be complete if we failed to acknowledge that strange, lonely pyramid he built in the woods in 1979 in

Pappas at Regency Square Branch Library, 1972, courtesy Ted
Pappas

the middle of suburban Arlington, loved and known as Tree Hill
Nature Center.

As the 1970s wilted into the exuberant next decade, an
environmental nonprofit contracted a likeminded architect to
build an apex to this hill. From the surrounding nature trails, you
spy the translucent pyramid rising through the longleaf pines and
sweetgum trees. Inside the Tree Hill Nature Center, dioramas and
displays spiral up a slight rise, floor by floor, until you reach the
apex, the single room featuring turtles and snakes and lizards at
the top.

From here, Ted's contemplative architecture merges into a subcategory of camps, behavioral and mental health "improvement" centers. Ironically, these designs, while connected to the vision in designing libraries and churches, take on more of the woodlands nature-based feel that Ted attributes to Broward's Unitarian Universalist Church of Jacksonville.

In Ted's Youth Development Center for Boys, now known as Duval Academy, on Ricker Road on Jacksonville's Westside; in his Camp Weed in Live Oak, Florida, now the Camp Weed and Cerveny Conference Center; and in the Duval Nassau Youth Camp, wooden interiors with flowing open spaces relate to the woods outside. From a distance, these buildings seem to rise like mounds of earth in A-frames and truncated pyramids.

Interiors of these designs share some of the same Pappas concepts and kinds of flow as his residential designs, most strongly with the

Pappas with Don Tredennick showing rendering of Youth Development Center for Boys, 1981, courtesy Ted Pappas

Katz Residence, Mom's Folly, and the Wilk House. Each structure incorporates outside light as much as possible, often from multiple levels. The Duval Nassau Youth Camp and Camp Weed, named for Reverend Edwin Gardner Weed, third Episcopal bishop of Florida, both let in light from above, a balcony or mezzanine, which then pours to an open lower level that itself brings the outside in. Similar elements occur in surprising other places, like the restaurant designs for Bennigan's Tavern on Jacksonville's Westside and Banjo's Restaurant at Regency Square in Arlington.

Meanwhile, the pyramid appears, mound-like without its apex, multiple times in the Youth Development Center and in different form altogether at the Duval Nassau Youth Camp. Out there, it stands atop a small knoll, taking shape from its hexagonal base full of windows. The second story cantilevers over the first with four wide sloping shingled eaves. Between each set of eaves stands a

Architectural model of Youth Development Center for Boys, 1981, courtesy Ted Pappas

central triangular window with two opposing triangles, one right side up, one upside down, either side. The result is a truncated pyramid rising out of a hexagon on a knoll, one form unfurling from another, the way natural shapes give rise to patterns.

Duval Nassau Youth Camp, 1980, courtesy Ted Pappas

Notes to Chapter Twelve

1.  Christy Pappas Gillam, in discussion with the author, May 2021.

2.  *Brick in Architecture* 37, no. 6 (December 1980): 4-5.

# Thirteen

## Northwest Jacksonville

Whereas Ted Pappas repurposed Epping Forest and was campus architect for the Bolles School for years in Southeast Jacksonville, he has also done extensive work throughout Northwest Jacksonville, from the urban core out to Edwards Waters College, Brentwood, and Moncrief. Bolles and Epping Forest are situated in some of the wealthiest and most predominantly white parts of the city, while Northwest Jacksonville is one of the most economically challenged parts of town and is largely African American. Pappas's work in Northwest Jacksonville started relatively early in his solo career with the Hogan's Creek Tower in 1976.

Meanwhile, not only has Pappas restored old structures and designed new buildings for the Bolles School, designed a prototype for Duval County Public Schools used for Crystal Springs Elementary and several other schools, and designed the swimming pool, dorms, and the Computer Science Building at the University of North Florida, but his relationship with Edward Waters College, the oldest historically black college in Florida, spans most of his career.

Pappas first worked with EWC in 1976. He designed an art gallery at the college's Centennial Hall in 1980. Some of his most important work at the college came along in 1987, when he restored the historic B. F. Lee Seminary Building, and in 1991, when he restored historic Centennial Hall itself. EWC is the oldest educational institution in Jacksonville and Centennial Hall is its signature building.

In 1916, when Edward Waters College built Centennial Hall, named to celebrate the African Methodist Episcopal Church's first hundred years, it contracted Richard Lewis Brown to build it and Howell and Stokes of Seattle to design it. John Mead Howell and Isaac Newton Phelps Stokes began their firm in 1897, focused on the Pacific Northwest and on educational buildings in general, and dissolved just after Centennial Hall. Howell and Stokes lasted twenty years, developing the Downtown Seattle site of the University of Washington, and designing buildings for the Pratt Institute in Brooklyn and St. Paul's Chapel at Columbia University in Manhattan. How they moved from working on elite schools in Providence, Rhode Island, and San Francisco to a struggling black institution in the Jim Crow South remains a mystery.

Centennial Hall at Edward Waters College, 1991, courtesy Ted Pappas

What Richard L. Brown, a black architect thought to have designed several structures in Jacksonville without getting his due, had to do with a Seattle architectural firm on its last leg, a firm who'd never before worked in the South and never worked for a segregated black institution, how Brown may have interacted with Howell and Stokes, and whether he played a role not just in construction but in design, remains material for a thousand educated guesses.

Brown was Jacksonville's first black architect. For certain structures for historically black use, Brown received credit for design, while for others he's listed only as builder. What he's credited with accomplishing is remarkable, since he was born a slave, and lends credibility to presuming successes for which he's *not* credited. City historians like Joel McEachin of the Jacksonville Historic Preservation Commission have wondered just what Brown's role may've been in the design and building of Centennial Hall.

Brown had worked as farmer, carpenter, and minister and served two terms as state representative during the Reconstruction boom of black political power in the 1880s. It seemed there was nothing he could not do. After the Great Fire of 1901 destroyed Edward Waters College buildings in central Jacksonville, the school board hired Brown as chief builder and repairman. Over the next decade, Brown oversaw construction of several new schools for which no architect was named. By this time, Jim Crow Laws were steadily undoing the advances of Reconstruction. It's surprising he got the job, but he'd proven he could do the work. It's less surprising he mightn't have received credit for original architectural designs.[1]

Brown is listed as both architect and builder for Mount Olive A.M.E. Church in Fairfield on Jacksonville's Eastside in 1922.[2] The school system would have appreciated his services, though not his name, his genius, or his color, in building the first two sections of Public School No. 8, built in 1909 and 1910; Fairfield School (School No. 9), built in 1910; and Lackawanna Elementary School

(School No. 10), built in 1911. He's listed only as builder for those schools, no architect named.[3]

When Pappas restored Centennial Hall in 1991, the college converted the building into its library. In contrast to the readily available funding for Bolles, Edward Waters College's funding, ever since its beginning a few years after the Civil War, has barely been enough to get it off life support. By the late 1980s, Centennial Hall's roof was caving in, all the windows needed replacement, and decades of flooding, since the building was situated low in relation to the ground around it, threatened to bring the building back into the earth.

Pappas first worked on the B. F. Lee Seminary Building across Old Kings Road from Centennial Hall in 1977, fully restoring it in 1991. The Lee Building, constructed from 1925 to '27, was designed by the prominent Jacksonville firm Marsh and Saxelbye, who also designed Bolles Hall, as the San Jose Hotel, and Epping Forest.[4] One thing Edward Waters *does* have in common with Bolles and Epping Forest is its continuum from Marsh and Saxelbye to Ted Pappas, a community architect truly grounded in every part of his hometown.

Pappas says the Lee Building, which had no air conditioning at the time, was in much better shape than Centennial Hall, a fact at least partly attributable to administrative offices having been located there. The interiors of the dorms on the fourth floor, however, needed a lot of attention. Centennial Hall may be EWC's flagship building, but B. F. Lee, with its dormer windows and Collegiate Gothic style of architecture, might be the college's most prestigious.

In the quad between the Lee and Tookes Buildings, you feel more like you're on a traditional college campus, walkable and integrated with the community, than at the University of North Florida, Jacksonville University, or any of the campuses of Florida State College at Jacksonville.

I travel with Ted and Mark around the brand-new football stadium, which Ted designed in 2020, to the Adams-Jenkins Sports and Music Complex, which Ted designed in 2004 and which opened in 2006. The complex features the sand tones Ted's used throughout his career and a grand portico fronted with seven massive columns topped with Prairie Style crosses. It was the first major construction project at Edward Waters in four decades. Talking about his long service to the school, Ted tries to count the EWC presidents he's worked for. He comes up with at least six. He's long served on the board of trustees and chaired the college's Institutional Advancement Committee under the school's previous president, former Duval County Sheriff Nat Glover.

Mark points out how Jacksonville could better emphasize its relationship with EWC, though its difficulties with funding over the years have paralleled challenges with accreditation and graduation rates. "The better Edward Waters College does, the better Jacksonville could do," he says. Were EWC to excel, it would lift the whole of Northwest Jacksonville and raise the status of the city itself. The obvious example would be Spelman College and Morehouse College, historically black colleges with excellent reputations. Spelman and Morehouse are sources of pride, prestige, and sophistication for Atlanta.

Also in the late 1980s, Ted Pappas designed the redevelopment of Brentwood, the city's first public housing project, where Jake Godbold, Jacksonville's mayor from 1978 to 1987, famously grew up. The new Brentwood development includes apartments, a senior center, and community center, and eliminated longstanding problems with flooding by raising the site and digging a retention basin.

It was through this work that Pappas developed a relationship with Paul Tutwiler, developer and director of the Northwest Jax Community Development Corporation. He developed a prototype for HabiJax housing, the Jacksonville chapter of Habitat for Humanity, the nonprofit organization that helps families build, rehabilitate, or preserve homes.

*151*

Tutwiler tells me, "I love and respect Ted Pappas not only for his talent and his vision, but for how he listens." Recalling community meetings, during which Ted listened to residents describe what they'd like to have in the ideal home, Tutwiler says Ted interacted graciously with the community and built a prototype according to its wishes. That prototype, featuring two stories and spacious porches, has now been used in the construction of dozens of houses around Moncrief Road and Myrtle Avenue North.

That relationship with Tutwiler, in turn, led to one of the most significant pieces of architecture and economic investment in this part of Northwest Jacksonville for years, the North Point Town Center at the convergence of Moncrief Road and Myrtle Avenue. These two roads, stretching long through northwest neighborhoods, meet in a large X on the map. At the northern juncture of this crossroads, terraced steps rise into the new village square. Or village triangle, rather.

"It's a beacon of hope," Tutwiler tells me. "It's about bringing our neighborhood back to life." North Point, he says, is the North Star of the community, even likening it to when slaves looked to the North as their hope for freedom. The town center would headquarter the CDC and serve as a small business incubator, with tenants including sandwich shops, barber shops, and beauty salons.[5]

Ted describes how the design dictated itself. "As I was sketching it out, I brought these angles together, then broke it up into slices," he says, "and that created this sawtooth effect for the roof." Being right at the northern point of Moncrief and Myrtle, which meet at an acute angle, the design had to address the triangle, just as a flatiron building would do.

As different as North Point Town Center is from a design like the Katz Residence, you can see a similar play with shapes, repetitions, and rhythms of form. An aerial view shows terraced steps rising from the corner, the five blades of the sawtooth rooftop rising from the terraces and facing the corner, each higher and wider than the

NORTH POINT TOWN CENTER
FOR
NORTH WEST JACKSONVILLE CDC.
JACKSONVILLE, FLORIDA

PBV ARCHITECTURE

North Point Town Center, 2014, courtesy Ted Pappas

one before it, then another rise into a two-story section, the whole structure a triangle pointing to the crossroads.

From the street level, the tall red stairwell and elevator tower contrasts to the rest of the center. "That's usually one of the most boring parts of a building," Ted says, "so we decided to make it red, curve the roof and make it stand out. It's like having an accent wall. It's a vertical element that separates the sawtooth from the rest of the building."

There's no greater advocate for Ted Pappas's architecture than his son, Mark. As much as he loves his father's architectural designs, he speaks as passionately of how much his father devoted his career to his community.

Addressing Ted one Friday across the conference table in their LaVilla offices, Mark says, "You've done projects at Clemson and the University of Florida, and you've done military base work, but your career has always been committed to Jacksonville. You could've gone elsewhere. You've had national connections with the American Institute of Architects, but you always did the bulk of your work here."

Mark says, "And I'm just thinking, big picture, your offices have always been downtown or in the urban core, Washington Street and Riverside Avenue and LaVilla, and you've done so much advisory work."

Oftentimes, Mark says, people take advisory work or work on a board, hoping to get the next affiliated job, but his father hasn't done that. He laughs that he hates "how Ayn Rand it sounds," but that Ted's very much "a citizen architect, a *Jacksonville* architect. Being part of the community and bettering the community has always been the drive."

I mention to Mark that Jacksonville businessman and artist, Steve Williams, once said, "Ted Pappas built Jacksonville." While Mark says that's a vast overstatement, that there's plenty of Jacksonville for which the Pappases wouldn't want to take credit, there's no part of town in which Ted hasn't grounded himself over his half-century-long career. You might not suspect the architect who'd repurposed Epping Forest from a residence to a yacht club had also served on the board for Edward Waters College and the Jacksonville Urban League. If Pappas was campus architect for the Bolles School, he came close to that designation for EWC, designing stadiums, galleries, sports complexes, and dorms, but also restoring the college's most important historic buildings.

Notes to Chapter Thirteen

1. Jacksonville Historic Landmarks Commission, *Jacksonville's Architectural Heritage* (Gainesville: University Press of Florida, 1989), 359.

2. Jacksonville Historic Landmarks Commission, *Jacksonville's Architectural Heritage* (Gainesville: University Press of Florida, 1989), 224.

3. Archives of Jacksonville Historic Preservation Commission.

4. Jacksonville Historic Landmarks Commission, *Jacksonville's Architectural Heritage* (Gainesville: University Press of Florida, 1989), 360.

5. Paul Tutwiler, in discussion with the author, May 2021.

# Fourteen

## Residences

Is it surprising when an architect does so much work over so long a career, but doesn't design his own residence? Jacksonville's other most famous architects—Henry John Klutho, William Morgan, Robert Broward, and Taylor Hardwick—all designed their own homes. Ted Pappas never did.

Mary Acree, the Pappases' first daughter, remembers the lot near her parents' first house in the Venetia neighborhood where Ted was going to design a house. Growing up loving the Mountain House, Mom's Folly, Mary imagined, as a child, the house her father would have designed in Venetia. Indeed, she designed it often enough in her own head.

"I had all these ideas," she says. "The bedrooms being up in the air. Living on the river. I was always imagining it."

Sometimes, when she was a child, Ted would compliment her drawing and say, "You might be an architect one day." Later, at the University of Georgia, she spent two years planning to major in interior design, before she realized it wasn't her forte. Now she's been a clinical social worker with Duval County Public Schools for more than three decades. After the Marjorie Stoneman Douglas High School Shooting in 2018, Duval County sent her south to help with the psychological aftermath in Parkland, Florida.[1]

As of this writing, Mary's sister Christy's youngest child, Grady, hopes to major in some kind of design when he starts college next year. "From when he was little," Christy says, "Grady would sit next to my dad or on my dad's lap, the two of them sketching together."[2]

There seems no definitive answer for why Ted Pappas never designed his own residence. Since he always loved working with historic architecture as much as designing his own, calling home a historic Mediterranean Revival style house designed by Marsh and Saxelbye made sense. Nevertheless, his contemporary residential designs have been as thoughtful and innovative as anything done by Hardwick or Broward.

Take the Katz Residence design. It looks both contemporary and very old. As so much of Ted Pappas's work looks back to ancient roots and forward in contemporary design, that shouldn't be surprising. Whereas his church designs and his influence by the Golden Mean, pyramids, and arches looks to the ancient past, however, the Katz House looks back to rustic beachfront Florida.

Katz Residence, 1974, courtesy Ted Pappas

It looks like it's been there for two hundred years but is also *avant-garde*.

Pappas situated the Katz House to its wild setting in a very different way than he situated Mom's Folly against its setting. In both cases, the design speaks to the wilderness surrounding it, but one house speaks to the mountains, the other to the harsh open setting of dunes, shifting sand, and ocean.

"The two settings are just the opposite," Ted says. "The Mountain House is surrounded. In the beach house, you're exposed. Looking out at the ocean, you can't see the end of the openness."

Ted Pappas knew attorney Harry Katz for most of his life. They knew each other from elementary school through high school. Katz grew up living in a bungalow in the Jewish section of Riverside near Post Street and Dellwood. Ted thought of him as a rebel.

Katz Residence, 1974, courtesy Ted Pappas

Katz wanted something "very anti-tradition," Ted says. He wanted "a house with no pretense, very open. He was interested in the spatial aspects inside, spatial contrasts." Here, once again, is the unfurling that occurs and recurs in Ted's designs. He could be describing Mom's Folly when he says, "It's open enough so that you could look across the room, look to the floor below, then look out to the ocean." Throughout, the design understates hardware like knobs, pulls, and hinges, because "Space becomes as essential as the solids."

So, the challenge of the Katz House was to discourse with the beach. Natural wood was necessary, cedar, rustic both inside and out, and left unpainted, sloped rafters exposed. Ted uses cedar and cypress frequently, because both woods weather well. "The beach is unforgiving," he says, noting that air conditioning units would need frequent replacement, because of the "havoc" wrought by the salt air.

Most of the beach houses along Route A1A through Ponte Vedra Beach now are "McMansions," Ted says. "They're saying, 'Look at me!' This house was the opposite." The Katz design worked from the inside out and brought the outside in. "It's more concerned with what you feel on the inside than what you look like on the outside."

That doesn't mean the Katz design isn't lovely, though. It may not announce itself, but it's a sight to behold. Writing and architecture share a number of concepts, and Ted speaks of the "poetry of shapes" the exterior design plays with. There's a rhythm of half a dozen rooftops of the same slope repeated at different heights and placements balanced against similarly sloped roofs facing elsewhere. Synesthetically, you hear the repetition, the rhythms in the placement of these shapes.

When Ted gets down deep in discussing particular design concepts, he says things like, "Finding the poetry in these spatial volumes is really exciting, because now you're dealing with the void." He says, "With space, you squeeze it and then you let it go."

As opposed to the Mom's Folly design, those repetitions and rhythms, punctuated with an aluminum rocket chimney instead of brick, become even more important against the invincible horizontal line that is the ocean. In Wright's Prairie Style of architecture, he "followed the earth line," and here, the Katz design responded to the oceanic horizon and the immensity of the blue sky.

Meanwhile, amidst the sand dunes and the sawgrass, the cedar takes on a golden color, most beautifully in the early waxing, or later fading, sunlight of spring and fall.

I use present tense to refer to the design itself, the platonic distinction I tried to make at the end of my discussion of the Hare Co./Milne-Pappas Building, but I cannot use present tense to refer to the house itself. It's been demolished, something the Pappases call a McMansion raised in its place. More and more, as I meet weekly with Ted and Mark, as I tour Ted's designs made manifest in the world, I marvel at the sharpness of his mind, his gracious and loving persona, his positive spirit, especially as I experience vicariously by his side his disappointment in how his designs have been altered over the years, or for what they've been demolished. If some sensitivity or thoughtfulness or attempt at awareness of what the architect had been after in his original vision had been evident in the alterations of his designs, that fact might have given Ted some solace. He's gracious enough to try to find it.

In a recent issue of Jacksonville's *Arbus* Magazine (a portmanteau word for arts and business, nothing to do with Diane Arbus), its annual issue focused on architecture, area architects answered the prompt, "Jacksonville has lost many of its historic buildings in recent years. Which remaining buildings (historic or recently built) do you think will or should survive for the next 50 years and why?" Embarrassingly, almost to the point of historical architectural illiteracy, R. Dean Scott, president of R. Dean Scott, Architect, Inc., said, "Few historically significant structures remain. Most residents would be hard-pressed to name more than one or two. Ironic, given our proximity to the nation's oldest city, St.

Augustine." I can name a couple hundred people who can name a couple hundred such structures.

More to the point, Ted Pappas said, "I'm at the point in my career where I have seen buildings that I designed torn down to make way for the next chapter. My heart (and ego) rarely agree with those decisions, be it a well-thought-out house with good form being demo'd to make way for a McMansion twice the size, or a church bulldozed to make way for apartments." He speaks of saving downtown riverfront space, rather than any particular historic structure, and mentions "world-class" parks on the river in great cities.[3]

When I search the ledger of Ted's architectural projects, consisting of thousands of projects but none later than 1995, I count more than seventy residential designs. At times, the fact that Ted has embodied the "citizen architect," rather than the "starchitect," elides the sheer number of significant designs he's brought to fruition. He's erudite, but humble, more interested in discussing arcane geometry and its historic spiritual significance than bragging about his achievements, and most of his residential designs over the decades he's simply moved on from and has a hard time recalling. Nevertheless, a few stand out.

Like the pyramid at Tree Hill, the A-frame of the Williams Residence built in 1979, which rises between West Jacksonville's Hillcrest and Hyde Park neighborhoods, seems born of its location in the trees. Built on a slight slope so that the back frame of the house is taller than the front, birches and pines reflect in the glass two and a half stories from the deck. The mirroring makes the trees appear twice the number that actually grow here, and the birches seem to proceed through the house to the other side. Even with this expanse of glass, though it invites the outside in, the overhanging steeply pitched eaves give the interior privacy.

Inside, the high cedar planking meets the trees so visible through the glass. The welcoming wood and wide stone fireplace make this house, in a very different way than the Katz Residence, feel both

Williams Residence, 1979, courtesy Ted Pappas

contemporary and ancient. Outside, wooden steps rise to decking that surrounds the tall triangle in the trees on all four sides.

These same shapes play differently in Pappas's Wilk Residence, built in 1988 in the Jacksonville suburb of Mandarin. From above, the earthen-colored brick house reveals itself to be a series of L's

Wilk Residence, 1988, courtesy Ted Pappas

laid one atop the other. On the ground, the termini of L's at the front, back, and north side appear as windowed prows with arched muntins beneath wide pitched eaves. One prow faces each compass direction, except to the south, where a two-story band of windows looks out from the family sitting area, stairs, and mezzanine, and to the west, where two prows point toward the river. The lower westward prow is one story tall, the height of each of the others, but the taller prow stands two stories tall and includes the master bedroom upstairs.

Those prows recall Ted's earlier design of Resurrection Catholic Church, but they also echo Frank Lloyd Wright's Unitarian Meeting House in Madison, Wisconsin. Wright referred to those muntins on the prow of the meeting house's belfry as hands coming together in prayer.

As Ted tours the house for the first time in three decades, he spies a nautilus decorating a shelf in the master bedroom and talks about how a house needs to build itself from the inside out. This house does that, from its wide spacious foyer just off its deep and wide, almost cavernous, front porch.

The house seems to reach an arm out in each direction, like a compass in circular motion, which is what that ancient symbol the swastika indicated, when cultures as diverse as Hindus and Navajos used it before Nazis perverted it forever. Of course, that compass in a wheel is also shaped like the nautilus.

The high-ceilinged room facing north, with prow window at one end and fireplace at the other, has most recently been used as a music room, as the piano by the prow attests. Inside the house, each prow window bears tall brick stanchions at either side. The smaller prow facing the river looks out from the dining room. The room with the prow facing east, at the front of the house, was originally designated the train room, as the original owner, James Wilk, kept his collection of model train sets there.

From the central family room, open from the ground floor to the top of the house with two-story floor-to-ceiling windows, an open-tread staircase leads to the second-floor landing with bedrooms to the side and the entrance to another corridor that leads to the master bedroom. It's quite an entrance. On either side of the corridor are bamboo screens for storage rooms. The walk ends in a wall that separates the corridor from the bedroom but doesn't reach the ceiling or the walls on either side.

When you come around the wall, either to the left or the right, the floor-to-ceiling prow window, nearly twenty feet tall, thrusts your view to the river and the dock that reaches out over it. Here, Ted, Mark, and I stand, looking at the river and speaking with Debbie Banks, who owns the house with her husband Garry Kitay, an orthopedic surgeon. The couple's three children are grown, so they're preparing the house they've called home for fifteen years for the market in order to downsize. They no longer feel they need 8,000 square feet.

Ted says that when James Wilk first approached him to build this house in the mid-1980s, Wilk wanted a Southern plantation-style house. Though Ted defines the architect as "creative interpreter" working for a client, he was able to sell Wilk on the idea of Frank Lloyd Wright's Prairie and Usonian style architecture. Finally, Wilk deferred.

I've been referring to the termini of the house "pointing" in compass directions, but Ted uses a better word, "thrust," a word that reminds me of the way he describes motion at work in Resurrection Catholic Church. It's not enough for architecture to point. It needs to move. Motion is an element, a material.

"You can see," he says, "how the spaces are thrust outwards to the exterior on an axis with the gable roofline. Not only is the outside brought in, but your vision is thrust to the outside." Again, he comes back to Wright and the Unitarian Meeting House. "Wright's interior spaces were extremely dynamic. Spaces were compressed and moved outward. There were surprises everywhere. When we refer to the destruction of the box, we imagine this image looking from the exterior onto the box. But the movement of the space is from the inside out."

Sounding on a theme that he's practiced his entire career, he says, "The majority of architecture is taking big boxes and breaking them into little boxes. We want to eliminate the boxes and set things in motion. It's about squeezing and shaping voids. It's the art of the in."

Notes to Chapter Thirteen

1.   Mary Pappas Acree, in discussion with the author, May 2021.

2.   Christy Pappas Gillam, in discussion with the author, May 2021.

3.   "25th Annual Art and Architecture Issue," *Arbus* Magazine, May/June 2021, 46.

# Epilogue

## 1. *The Stones*

You can't see the stones from the road. I park at the Doty Building, where Ted Pappas first opened his solo offices in his Uncle John's building in 1968, then walk a block north on Washington Street. I pass one of the closed ramps to the Isaiah D. Hart Bridge, each of the ramps scheduled for demolition, and walk east on Monroe Street.

This portion of Downtown still retains ghost shadows of its original neighborhood feel. Perhaps a hundred of the thousands of original tall, handsome houses with spacious porches, like the prototype Ted designed for Northwest Jacksonville HabiJax after listening to community concerns and dreams, still stand. Attorneys and bail bondsmen operate offices in the structures that aren't boarded-up rooming houses. Lots of empty lots hold the absence of lovely homes demolished. A present absence. A what-should-have-been had Jacksonville, as every other North American city, not ruined so much of itself.

In just such a block, I pass a gaggle of homeless men and women who've parked their shopping carts in a space central to their assemblage. Across the street, a broken-down 1970s van bears a Georgia license plate and flat tires. The jail's a block over. So's the Sulzbacher Homeless Center. The police headquarters is two blocks away. Clearly homelessness, failure at basic survival and citizenship, is still linked directly to criminality, just as vagrancy laws, not so long ago in this country, illegalized people police perceived to be in the wrong place.

I walk deep into a vacant lot. The lot runs deeper than you'd think from the street. From a broken chain-link gate at the back of the lot, I enter what I think of as the final resting place for the Milne-Pappas Building: its ruins, its boneyard, but also its Ship of Theseus.

## 2. Not Just a Memory

Mary Lee Pappas says she doubts Ted thinks about how his architecture will be remembered in the future. "I think it would be painful," she says. "He's received so many design awards over the years that I can't even remember how many he's won, but so often, we've seen his buildings come and then go. It's the same with Bob Broward and Bill Morgan. And these days, architects do more holistic city planning, but Jacksonville still hasn't gotten to that point. Even though he's talked about it, and been asked his views about it, for as long as I can remember. I think his biggest frustration has been the lack of vision."[1]

While Ted may not think of his career in terms of future heritage, more than one of his designs is slated for inclusion in the upgraded version of a tome called Jacksonville's Architectural Heritage. The first edition of the book, featuring descriptions and photographs of thousands of architecturally and historically significant structures, a project undertaken by activists like Wayne Wood and historians like Joel McEachin for the Jacksonville Historic Landmarks Commission, was published in 1989. Though a back section called "Four for the Future" included the Singleton Senior Center, one of the criteria for inclusion was that a building be at least fifty years old. When the second edition is published for Jacksonville's bicentennial in 2022, it will include several Pappas designs, most prominent among them St. John the Divine.[2]

Even after watching the destruction of his heart- and headquarters, however, Ted didn't give up. On April 10, 2002, the Times-Union's Sandy Strickland wrote, "About four weeks ago, Jacksonville architect Ted Pappas moved out of a historic building on Riverside Avenue that was to be demolished to make way for the road's widening."

She continued, "He made sure, however, that the building's striking façade, made of 150-pound stones, wouldn't become just a memory." He'd fought the demolition for a decade and succumbed to the vision of its fatality years ago, but a month prior to his HQ's destruction, he removed its great stone blocks, planning to reinstate them elsewhere. He'd received an estimate that it would cost a million dollars, which he could not afford, to move what certainly seemed now his most important building, "so instead he got a special permit to save what he could of the exterior."

The Florida D.O.T. called the procedure abnormal, said "typically" a "contractor" would "dispose" of a structure that stood in the way of eminent domain "in the most expedient way possible, usually in an approved landfill," but spokesmen said this building was "different" and "special" and "significant."

Strickland referred to "the architect," and his work at "Epping Forest Yacht Club" and "the Beaches Library" and "First Guaranty Bank," as having "hoped to remove the framework and decorative pediment," which he "couldn't [do] without structurally impacting the building," which he noted, ironically, "I'm not authorized to do."[3]

Where Ted moved the stones, what he planned to do, and how those plans fell through with the continued sinking of his broken heart, I, for the longest time, don't know. It's as big a mystery as what Taylor Hardwick did with the onion domes he salvaged from the destruction of the original St. John the Divine Greek Orthodox Church downtown.

## 3. *The Vision*

In the early 2000s, Preston Haskell was, depending on whom you speak with, the third or fourth most powerful person in Jacksonville. Though Jacksonville Transit Authority engineers originally drew up plans to expand Riverside Avenue toward the river side, Haskell convinced the City to alter its plans inland, what Ted still calls "our side of the street."

Haskell justified this change, and city officials ultimately agreed, by saying the plan protected the old YMCA Building and the historic Brooklyn Fire Station #5 from demolition. Since the widening of Riverside Avenue demolished the Milne-Pappas Building and other historic structures on the inland side, both the original YMCA Building and the fire station have been demolished and engineers have asked the JTA and the Florida Department of Transportation to consider spending money to narrow this section of Riverside Avenue yet again to make it more friendly for new urban neighborhood construction.

When I ask Ted what he did with the stones following the demolition, he says, "That was a quick emotional decision. To reuse those stones would require special planning and design and a special-use building. That opportunity never happened."

"The stones," he tells me, "are on an empty lot on Monroe Street near Washington. I have since sold the lot to Alex Sifakis, local developer. It cost me $13,000 to move the stones in the year 2000. I couldn't see spending that much and more again. Perhaps Alex will find a good use. Maybe a mausoleum."

I find the stones at the back of a lot off Monroe. A broken gate leads to a lot behind a lot. Here lie the stones, four and five and six deep, in three long rows, and in dismantled piles, grown over by woodbine and greenbriar. Standing here is a strangely emotional experience. I could wait one thousand years for the earth to usurp and welcome us over.

What might I now say? I suppose I argue for the value of an architectural design even against whether it's been built, been respected since built, or even still stands, because I'm a writer. I don't have to build anything. I don't have to build anything physical. I chronicle ideas as they happen in the world in the best edifices of words I can erect. An architect may be, as Ted often says, a "creative interpreter," but Ted Pappas is also a man with his own ideas and vision. The designs themselves exist yet, and will still, and must.

Consider the Ship of Theseus and Grandfather's Axe. These are the names of two versions of the same thought experiment. If you replace one part of the ship, it's still the same ship, right? What if you keep replacing parts of the ship until, over time, you've replaced every single original piece? Does the original ship no longer exist? Or is it still the same ship?

With Grandfather's Axe, if you replace the handle, it's still the same axe, right? What if you later replace the head of the axe, too? Is it the same axe as when you replaced the handle, but not the same axe you started with? Or is Grandfather's Axe always Grandfather's Axe?

It stings the designer to witness these alterations, because the building is the representation of his design in the world. No one, however, can remodel his original vision. In the Beginning was the Word. That's the design behind. Always a rose is a rose is a rose. Then again, a thing in the world exists in the world.

I doubt Alex Sifakis will build a mausoleum of the one-hundred-fifty-pound stones from the demolished Milne-Pappas Building, but I also doubt Ted meant that comment any way but sardonically. I imagine a space, created entirely of words, words as the most ephemeral material, in which those stones would find a good use, maybe even a space I could write, maybe even a space I'm writing right now and that you're reading. If so, hope I could do it some slightest semblance of justice.

Ted Pappas in his then-new headquarters at 100 Riverside Avenue, December 1980, photo by Gary Parker, courtesy *Florida Times-Union*

Notes to Epilogue

1.  Mary Lee Pappas (wife), in discussion with the author, May 2021.

2.  Jacksonville Historic Landmarks Commission, *Jacksonville's Architectural Heritage* (Gainesville: University Press of Florida, 1989), 383.

3.  Sandy Strickland, "Architect Saves Stones from Historic Building," *Florida Times-Union* (Jacksonville, FL), April 10, 2002.

# Architectural Citizenship

### by Mark Pappas

## 1. *Citizen Architect*

In Ayn Rand's 1943 novel *The Fountainhead*, the Frank Lloyd Wright-inspired character Howard Roark often finds himself up against "the crowd," facing down critics and conformists, while embracing his true self at all costs. Most architects can relate on some level to the individualism that Roark embraces; imagine a world with boundless commissions where architects are given free rein to create as they will. Yet the bombastic novel is full of blathering rhetoric about the self. "All that which proceeds from man's independent ego is good. All that which proceeds from man's dependence upon men is evil."

Except that it's not. At least not in the world of Ted Pappas. Architecture, as practiced and preached by Pappas, is the process whereby the architect uses his skill and artistry to bring a vision to life, to interpret the client's functional needs into a hopefully pleasing form. The idea that this is accomplished as an individual act is outside the realm of reality. Your team of architects and draftsmen work to pull your interpretation together. The structural engineer calculates how to make your creation stand the stresses of gravity. The electrical engineer brings life to the building while the mechanical and plumbing engineers work to keep it alive. And so on.

Yet it begins much earlier than all that. With education and learning. Becoming inspired by working through the challenges of those who came before you. Through being mentored and eventually mentoring.

It was early in Ted's career that he realized education and inspiration needed to continue beyond those early days of long hours in the project room at Clemson, of suffering through the physics and calculus that are part of the day-to-day life of an architect. Ted's early employers and mentors provided wisdom and guidance that would travel with him throughout his career. And it was this inspiration that he received from working and learning and struggling and laughing with his contemporaries that drove him to find the means to make that part of his life.

Ted joined the American Institute of Architects in 1964. This was a time of fewer architects, so in theory less competition. In truth being a part of the institute on a local level was very much about the camaraderie amongst peers, and a way of keeping up with what others in your immediate sphere were doing. To be a part of the AIA was a way for young architects to engage with the local legends, to learn from them, and for Pappas, a way to better understand the business of the profession.

They did not teach much of the business at the Clemson School of Architecture in the 1950s, or much anywhere else for that matter. Like many aspects of real life, one was expected to learn the painful truths of business from actual experience. To be worked fourteen-hour days as a draftsman at the big firm; to be shared among the egos of the May Street School like a minor league baseball player, to get squeezed dry by the local developer until you had nothing left to give—that is how Ted learned the business.

So the AIA became a refuge for Ted. A place to learn about new techniques, to lend and receive a sympathetic ear, and to find partners to work with. Eventually he would expand his horizons to the Florida chapter. The state conventions offered even more opportunity to explore, and with less of the competition that comes at the local level. After spending time in various leadership roles at AIA Jacksonville, he rose to chapter president in 1977. By 1981 he had risen to president of the Florida Association. Under Ted's leadership, the stranglehold South Florida had on the state chapter was challenged at a time of internal strife, and the headquarters moved from Miami to Tallahassee. The capital city seemed an appropriate location from which to influence the whole of Florida. Ted was instrumental in creating a place for the AIA in Tallahassee and as chairman of the Capital Center Planning Commission, which oversaw how the myriad public buildings in Downtown Tallahassee were developed and coordinated.

## 2. Mr. President

The Florida-Caribbean AIA soon elected Ted Pappas to the AIA Board of Directors, where he served a three-year term. While serving on the board, he was commissioner for the Technical Committee and a member of the Media Advisory Committee. Eventually, he was elected vice president of AIA National for 1985. At the 1986 convention in San Antonio, Ted was elected first vice president/president-elect. He was inaugurated as the Institute's 64th president in December 1987 at the Organization of American States.

The demand on Ted's time in the AIA was significant. He traveled weekly around the country and to three continents as an ambassador for the American profession. After a thirty-six-hour journey to the South Island of New Zealand, a weary Ted Pappas, wife, and son enjoyed a jet-lagged dinner among the top architects of the country. A senior official kindly explained, in light of the recent global economic recession, that "When the United States sneezes, the rest of the world gets pneumonia."

The architect embraced the national stage as a grand opportunity. Not for himself, but for the profession. As an article for the *Engineering News-Record* said, "Everyone likes Ted Pappas. He's known as a solid individual with an unbelievable amount of energy.

But his enthusiasm is so low-key that even people he is organizing don't know they're being organized." The article noted his primary goal for the year: "Pappas would like to see a public awareness of the architect as the Renaissance man, who can integrate art, business and technology."[1]

The centerpiece of Ted's time as AIA national president was the long-term planning initiative, Vision 2000. This effort brought together a diverse group of experts to look at the changes looming in the coming century related to technology, demographics, and culture. In explaining the project, Ted said, "Once we reduce the uncertainty of the future, architects can position themselves as leaders and help shape it."[2]

In 1988 the American Institute of Architects held a joint conference with the Royal Institute of British Architects in Pittsburgh focused on remaking cities, a focus that Ted sought to implement back home in Jacksonville throughout his career. At the conference, Ted said, "The challenge for architects is to get out of their offices and into the community. The challenge for the community is to stop waiting for a white knight or 'master builder' and to take charge of its own future." Prince Charles, a great aficionado of architecture, gave the closing address at the conference, urging the profession to create public places of great

Ted Pappas, Prince Charles, and other dignitaries, Vision 2000, 1988, photo by Ben Spiegel

interest and to go beyond functionalism by "embellishing building for man's pleasure and for the sheer joy in beauty itself."

Back home in Jacksonville, Ted was challenged to keep his thriving office going with the many demands on his time. His loyal and hard-working staff was up to the challenge, even against the realities of business. While reaching the top of the professional association was a feat to be celebrated locally, and it was, it was also a chance for his competitors to try to gain an edge against him and his "national focus." Far from being deterred, Ted believed that promoting the profession at home, on the national stage, and abroad was worth every long flight, every pre-Zoom team meeting at 10:00 p.m. over the phone.

For Ted, to be able to work with thought leaders at the state and national level was an incredible opportunity. To put aside competition for the local Request for Proposals and engage with the likes of Faye Jones, Santiago Calatrava, and Kenzo Tange was an opportunity he could not have imagined when he first stepped onto that bus to Clemson University in 1952.

## 3. *Fellowship*

To be elevated to the AIA College of Fellows is to receive the AIA's highest membership honor based on an individual's exceptional work and contributions to architecture and society. Only three percent of AIA members achieve this distinction. Ted Pappas received his fellowship in 1982 at the AIA National Convention in Honolulu, Hawaii, at the Blaisdell Concert Hall in front of family and colleagues. It was a proud moment, a distinction based on achievements in design, public service, and historic preservation. It's even more challenging for the head of a small firm to give the time and effort to afford such a distinction.

That is what drives Ted Pappas. To be a part of things bigger than himself. Later in his career, as one of only a handful of AIA fellows in Jacksonville, Ted was asked to lead a workshop

Ted Pappas speaking at his American Institute of Architects
presidential inauguration, 1987, courtesy American Institute of
Architects

for AIA Jacksonville to help others understand the process and significance of fellowship. After a presentation focusing on how his own experience led to receiving his fellowship, a participant asked what benefits he had received as a result. Ted was stumped (not a common position for him); he didn't have a good answer. Did it mean more business, more awards? If that wasn't it, what was it then? It was simply a moment, a confirmation amongst the stresses of running a firm, of working on the next study, of providing guidance, that he was on the right path for his vision of what an architect should be. Don't do it expecting some great windfall, Ted stated. Maybe that will be your luck. But becoming the complete architect one wants to be is reason enough. Ted would live up to this ideal with the College of Fellowship itself, eventually being elected to the Executive Committee of the College of Fellows. In 2006 he served as its chancellor.

Following his presidency, Pappas found himself pulled to continue bringing his leadership to a number of institutions. He served on the Board of Regents of the American Architectural Foundation, the philanthropic arm of the AIA that seeks to inspire and attract the next generation of architects.

Traveling the country and the world was an exciting time for the Pappas family. They went to the Olympics in Canada, visited Australia, New Zealand, and Japan, saw incredible architecture, and met amazing people. What may have energized Ted Pappas more than any other leadership responsibility, however, was his engagement with higher education.

### 4. *Higher Education / Architectural Accreditation Board*

Ted Pappas is a lifetime learner. Never one to golf or take time at the country club, he is most at home in a bookstore or at home reading or scouring the internet. A quick scan of his search history will find hundreds of aerial images of rice terraces in Asia and South America and the rise and fall of cities. He's an avid scholar of the Bible, and you will likely find challenging if not distressing textbooks in the stack by his favorite chair.

He embraced the opportunity to explore, engage, and assist higher educational facilities when he joined the National Architectural Accrediting Board, the organization that develops and maintains the accreditation system in professional degree programs. Ted participated in eighteen accreditation visits to various universities, including Virginia Tech, Cornell University, Yale University, and the University of Florida.

Ted's NAAB accreditation visits were intense, focused efforts to dig into an architectural program, understand how they worked (or didn't), and work with administrators to improve them. It's a little surprising that Ted didn't end up full time in higher ed at some point, teaching students how to handle that slick contractor looking to blow up the budget or wrangle the engineers from mucking up the design. In 1992 a Chinese delegation viewing the accreditation visit at Catholic University School of Architecture in Washington, D.C., offered Ted an opportunity to join a university administration in China.

Pappas also served on the advisory council at the University of Florida, Mars Hill University, and at his alma mater, Clemson University, where he has served on the President's Advisory Committee, the Architectural Advisory Committee, and the Board of Visitors.

## 5. *The Sense of Place*

Speaking of the first man to discover how to make fire, Ayn Rand laments, "He was probably burnt at the stake he'd taught his brothers to light, but he left them a gift they had not conceived, and he lifted darkness from the face of the Earth." Ted Pappas may not have created fire, but his impact on his profession, his community, his contemporaries, and family have brought forth a light that shines brightly and will for years and decades to come.

While his influence may have extended to faraway lands, his primary focus has been and always will be on his hometown of Jacksonville, Florida. A member and often leader of countless boards and institutions, Ted has worked with a diverse group of civic organizations, including the Jacksonville Urban League, Greenscape, Operation New Hope, Edward Waters College, the March of Dimes, JaxPride, and the think tank Jacksonville Community Council Inc.

These were investments of his time, leadership, and expertise with the primary goal of improving the city that is his home, self-serving only in the sense that he wants to see things improve for all. And while that philosophy certainly pertains to his architecture, getting the next commission was never the reason to become an involved and engaged citizen. Responding to a local arts magazine's annual architecture issue, Ted was asked to provide a recent project to profile. Rather than show a new building or residence, Ted took the opportunity to promote a riverfront greenspace concept he's working on. Ted says, "As an architect, I design structures: offices, churches, schools, houses, and buildings of all sorts. Of equal importance to the vertical construction of a project is its sense of place, how it connects to the site, how it addresses and looks to nature for inspiration and direction. And while every project doesn't begin with a blank canvas amidst nature, it is incumbent on the architect to constantly strive to find those unique opportunities within our communities. So one of my most intense focuses has been not on a building or one of my own projects."[3]

This has been the case for much of his career during the past thirty years. In the 1990s Ted developed a "Central Park Concept" that centered around some of Downtown Jacksonville's greatest architecture in the form of historic churches along Duval Street. Having developed two detailed models of Downtown Jacksonville, Ted touted this plan to mayors and council members. It was voted a top project in Jacksonville's inaugural OneSpark Festival of Ideas in 2013. To this day, Ted continues to seek ways to make this project happen.

Endnotes

1. R. Randall Vosbeck, Tony P. Wrenn, and Andrew Brodie Smith, *A Legacy of Leadership: The Presidents of the American Institute of Architects, 1857–2007*, (Washington, D. C.: The American Institute of Architects, 2008), 172-74.

2. Vosbeck, Wrenn, and Smith, *A Legacy of Leadership*, 172-74.

3. "AIA Jacksonville 2021," *Arbus Magazine*, May/June 2021.

# Index